The CENTRAL WALES LINE

D1792845

The CENTRAL WALES LINE

Rheilffordd Canol Cymru

Tom Clift

LONDON

IAN ALLAN LTD

First published 1982

ISBN 0 7110 1204 0

All rights reserved. No part of this book may be reproduced or transmitted in any form or by any means, electronic or mechanical, including photocopying, recording or by any information storage and retrieval system, without permission from the Publisher in writing.

© Ian Allan Ltd 1982

Published by Ian Allan Ltd, Shepperton, Surrey; and printed by Ian Allan Printing Ltd at their works at Coombelands in Runnymede, England

Contents

Introduction

'PASSENGERS ARE REQUESTED to ask for tickets by the LMS route, that being the shortest and most expeditious between South and Central Wales and Manchester, Liverpool and other important cities and towns in the North of England.'

This 'suggestion' accompanied LNWR and LMS timetables for the Central Wales Line from Swansea to Shrewsbury, which, though a shadow of its former self, still provides passengers with a short and expeditious path across the Welsh interior.

Various factors combine to make this line rather special: its length, scenery, atmosphere, history (and present, if somewhat tenuous, existence). On a map the route is shown as an almost straight line from its respective termini. Between them is 120 miles of rapidly varying picturesque scenery, sometimes breathtaking, and always interesting. A journey from Carmarthen to Crewe via 'the Central' is $163\frac{1}{2}$ miles (and before the direct line to Llandilo closed was $147\frac{3}{4}$ miles); via Hereford it is $216\frac{1}{2}$ miles; or 241 miles via Birmingham. No one in their right mind would take the longer routes by choice if offered equal quality of service via Central Wales, if only because of the view out of the window. From Llanelli there is the Loughor Valley as far as Ammanford and Tirydail, along with the industrial horizons of Trostre tinplate works, Morlais Colliery and Wernos Washery. Then there is the tortuous descent through the woods between Derwydd Road and Ffairfach, which is reminiscent of a West Country branch line. Llandilo stands above the railway on one side, with the River Towy on the other, and it is up this wide, flat valley that the line proceeds to Llandovery, where the more spectacular scenery and hillclimbing starts, as the countryside becomes more isolated. Up the famous bank to Sugar Loaf where South Wales ends and Central Wales begins, and the weather so often changes after passing through the tunnel. Into 'Spa country' the track heads towards a crossing of Wales' premier river, the Wye, at Builth Road (roughly halfway) before climbing to Llandrindod Wells and beyond, to the line's peak at lonely Llangunllo (miles from anywhere and 980ft up). Down towards the River Teme, which is crossed at Panpunton Bridge (a mile before Knighton) taking the line out of Wales and into gentler English terrain for the final 12 miles to Craven Arms, the junction with the Newport-Hereford-Shrewsbury-Crewe route.

Every couple of miles the scene changes. Just in the same way that Swansea and Shrewsbury are worlds apart, the same can be said about Pontardulais and Llandilo, or Llangadog and Llangammarch, or Dolau and Bucknell. A detailed appreciation of the scenery mile by mile can be gained from the *Heart of Wales Line* booklet produced by BR (Western Region) with AvonAnglia Publications. Similarly, the complex history of the route is chronicled in D. J. Smith's *Shrewsbury to Swansea* (Town and Country Press). In brief, the line's historical development was the result of small companies ploughing into the hinterland from both ends. The various sections were opened thus:

1839	Llanelli to Pontardulais	
1841	Pantyffynnon to Ammanford & Tirydail	
1857	Ammanford & Tirydail to Llandilo	
	(all constructed by the Llanelly Dock & Railway Company)	
1858	Llandilo to Llandovery (Vale of Towy Railway)	
1860	Craven Arms to Bucknell	(Knighton Railway)
1861	Bucknell to Knighton	(Knighton Railway)
1862	Knighton to Knucklas	(Central Wales Railway)
1864	Knucklas to Penybont	(Central Wales Railway)
1865	Penybont to Llandrindod Wells	(Central Wales Railway)
1866	Llandrindod Wells to Builth Road	(Central Wales Extension Railway)
1867	Builth Road to Llanwrtyd Wells	(Central Wales Extension Railway)
1867	Pontardulais to Swansea Victoria	(Llanelly Dock & Railway Company)
1868	Llanwrtyd Wells to Llandovery	(Central Wales Extension Railway)

By the time the cross-country link was forged in 1868 the London & North Western Railway had absorbed the Knighton, Central Wales and Central Wales Extension Railways. The Vale of Towy Railway was shared by the LNWR and Llanelly Railway, whilst the LNWR won a legal battle in the House of Lords giving it control of the Llanelly Railway's Pontardulais-Swansea section from 1871. The Llanelly Railway's half share in the Vale of Towy and its control of the Llandilo-Llanelli segment became the responsibility of the Great Western Railway. Hence the joint nature of the line.

Of the complete journey of $115\frac{3}{4}$ miles from Swansea Victoria to Shrewsbury, 62% was on LNWR (LMS post-1923) owned track, 11% was GWR territory (with LNWR/LMS running powers) and 27% of the route was shared between the two major Companies, including, of course, the 20 miles between Craven Arms and Shrewsbury.

Following Nationalisation in 1948, the line became part of the Western Region of British Railways, much to the displeasure of the predominantly LNWR/LMS staff. In 1962, and again in 1967, the Western Region proposed closure of the route. In 1964 the line was reprieved between Llanelli and Craven Arms by the Minister of Transport on the grounds that hardship to the local population would be caused by closure. The section from Swansea Victoria to Pontardulais closed on 13 June 1964. Again in 1969 the line was retained by the Transport Minister — the official reason was, once more, that considerable hardship would be caused if closure took place. Now it is said that Richard Marsh, the Transport Minister at the time, provided the Cabinet with a 'cast iron' case for closing the route, but that the decision was reversed when George Thomas, the then Secretary of State for Wales, pointed out that the line ran through several marginal constituencies! Suffice to say that the natives get very restless when anyone mentions possible withdrawal of their only comprehensive form of public transport.

It is physically impossible to provide an adequate replacement bus service. North of Llandovery a bus is something which runs maybe a couple of times a week to the major towns from the outlying villages. The only daily long distance buses run across the route of the railway. It was once calculated that to travel from Swansea to Shrewsbury via the bus services that run parallel to the railway would take over a week! On the few occasions when a bus has had to be hastily summoned to replace a failed train en route the resultant delay to passengers and damage to the bus driver's state of mind have been considerable — pity the poor man trying to negotiate single tracked lanes in his attempt to serve the inhabitants of Llangunllo or Cynghordy. On one occasion a bus took $3\frac{1}{2}$ hours to get from Llandrindod Wells to Shrewsbury, and even then some of the halts were by-passed. On one summer Saturday, due to chronic over-crowding on the 09.59 Swansea-Shrewsbury dmu, a bus was hired to run from Llandrindod to Shrewsbury (calling only at Knighton) as a relief to the train. At Llandrindod the passengers crammed into the dmu were told a bus was waiting outside which would offer them seats and serenity. Yet, despite the chronic conditions in the train, the bus left with only five people aboard!

It is unfortunate that so many cross-country lines that passed from one pre-Nationalisation company into the hands of a different post-Nationalisation region of BR have suffered at their new owner's hands. One thinks of the former Southern lines in the West Country, or the Somerset & Dorset, or the former Great Western lines between Birmingham Snow Hill and North Wales. As a result of what has happened to the Central Wales Line there has been, in recent decades, considerable anti-Western feeling. Before the run down the Western faction was looked on with a sort of patronising contempt, with its local trains hauled by small tank engines. However, the attitude hardened and changed when the LMS position of superiority ended after Nationalisation. The feeling was that the new masters were deliberately running down their former opponents' line in order to close it. This view still prevails today, over 33 years after Nationalisation, though you will probably see from the pictures in this book why such an attitude has been fostered.

Some of this 'anti-Westernism' probably has a justifiable basis, but there are also amusing misconceptions. On several occasions I have been told that the real reason for the powerful spotlight on the front of Central Wales trains is to prevent 'Western' men getting lost in the dark! Similarly, when Port Talbot panel box was extended to control Central Wales trains between Swansea High Street, Llanelli and Pantyffynnon, it was alleged that the 'Western' men in the box were giving preference to their coal trains over 'Midland' passenger trains!

This atmosphere has bred fiercely independent railwaymen who run the line responsibly on a daily basis in isolation from the rest of the BR system. Not that this attitude is solely confined to the railway community. There is the example of an AA man who, seeing a dmu failed at Llandrindod Wells, with the driver and guard attempting a temporary repair, offered his services — free of charge! My Grandfather, when he lived near the railway at Howey, used the passage of the up Swansea-York Mail as his signal to retire for the night.

Though the line today differs from that of the past, the most important changes took place within the two years 1964 and 1965. In those years diesel replaced steam, through freights disappeared, most stations were unstaffed, and passing loops closed. Thus, within a couple of years, the character and role of the line changed completely, from being an important cross-country route to a Light Railway. It is also worth noting that before this period of change things stayed very much the same for decades. The timetable did not alter significantly, the same engines were used — not just the same class, but the same members of those classes. Since the mid-1960s little has altered; there was the revised service to and from Swansea High Street after May 1970, which looks not dissimilar to the basic five each way service which ran between Swansea and Shrewsbury before 1964. Trains now leave Swansea High Street at 05.44; 10.08; 12.25; 15.00 and 19.05. Twenty years ago trains to Shrewsbury departed from Swansea Victoria at 06.15; 07.25; 10.25; 12.20 and 18.25. In 1928 the times were 05.40; 07.45; 10.15; 12.35; 14.35 and 18.35. In 1885 trains left at 06.15; 10.00; 12.30 and 17.00.

As regards the basic pattern of services, in addition to the Swansea-Shrewsbury train, there were the local services between Llanelli and Llandovery, Swansea Victoria and Pontardulais, and some short workings between Llandovery, Builth Road, Llandrindod Wells, Knighton and Craven Arms, some of which were related to market days.

On the freight side, in addition to an abundance of local activity at the south end of the line especially, there were express freights using the route throughout the 24 hours to and from yards in the North of England and the Midlands.

With regard to the resources used in running these trains, engine power came from LMS sheds at Swansea Paxton Street and Shrewsbury, as well as assistance from smaller sheds at Llandovery, Builth Road, Knighton and Craven Arms. The GWR had depots at Llanelli, Pantyffynnon and Llandovery. Many of the engines used spent several years working over the route. This feature has continued since 'dieselisation' as the dmus used have to be fitted with spotlights for the now numerous ungated level crossings, and consequently, the same sets are consistently used.

Trainmen were provided from the depots mentioned above. For a time there was a turn for a Crewe guard over the route who used to work the last down passenger train from Shrewsbury as far as Garth, from where he used to return with the Swansea and Milford fish train to Crewe.

In addition to various out and back workings from the major depots there were also a few lodging turns involving men staying overnight before returning home the next day. During fine weather Salop crews were known to have slept rough in a field between the railway and the river at Llandovery.

This then is the background to the views of the 'Central' which follow. Most of the material was taken in the years up to 1964. There are a few ancient shots included, as well as several contemporary photographs for the sake of historical comparison and interest. The choice of photographs has been based chiefly on availability; despite its interest value the line (especially at the south end) has not been as well photographed as one might have expected.

The layout of the book has been designed to give an impression of the line from Swansea Victoria up the route to Craven Arms and Shrewsbury. At the conclusion of the main section is an appendix devoted to the branch lines off the main route from Llanmorlais, Llanelli, Brynamman/Gwaun-cae-Gurwen/Abernant and Carmarthen.

Throughout I have used 'up' to mean towards Shrewsbury, and 'down' conversely towards Swansea. Similarly 'north' of a particular location means nearer Shrewsbury, even though, strictly speaking, the line runs in a generally north-easterly direction though, in isolated areas (notably between Llanbister Road and Knighton) its specific direction varies considerably. I have used the anglicised place names which applied at the time when most of the photographs were taken. A process of bilingualisation is now under way and, therefore, some of the spellings used herein do not correspond to the correct Welsh versions now being used by BR.

Acknowledgements

Without the assistance of numerous good folk this book would obviously not have taken shape and so, with considerable gratitude and best wishes, I would like to thank the following for taking the time to help me:

Meirion Baldwin; C. R. Berridge; Mrs S. M. Byrne; Miss M. Cadwallader; W. A. Camwell; H. C. Casserley; D. J. Clarke; David and Derek Cross; Emrys Davies; Hugh Davies; Michael Denman; Dr Richard Gulliver; Miss N. Haswell; G. A. Hookham; Terry Dyddgen Jones; D. A. Idle; Lens of Sutton; John Lewis; Dr James McGregor; David Mathew; the late Ernest Morgan; Sid Morris; Roy Palmer; Miss Perkins; Powys' County Librarian and Planning Officer; M. G. Rayner; Real Photographs Ltd; R. F. Roberts; David Rowe, J. A. Smith; John Stratton; Glyn and Michael Watson.

I am especially grateful to the suppliers of the photographic material and caption information and to the numerous railwaymen, who by conversing about the line with me have provided inspiration. I would also like to thank members of the PROs organisation at Paddington and Neil Sprinks, the Cardiff Division PRO.

I hope that those who know 'the Central' will feel that this photographic record does the line justice, and, more importantly, I hope that between them, Government (both National and Local) and BR, assisted by the newly formed Heart of Wales Line Travellers Association, will ensure that the opportunity to travel through the Welsh heartland by this 'most expeditious' cross country railway will be available for the foreseeable future.

Tom Clift
June 1982

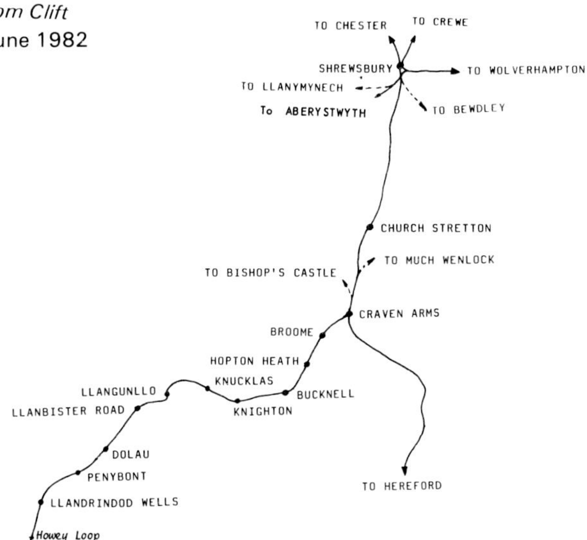

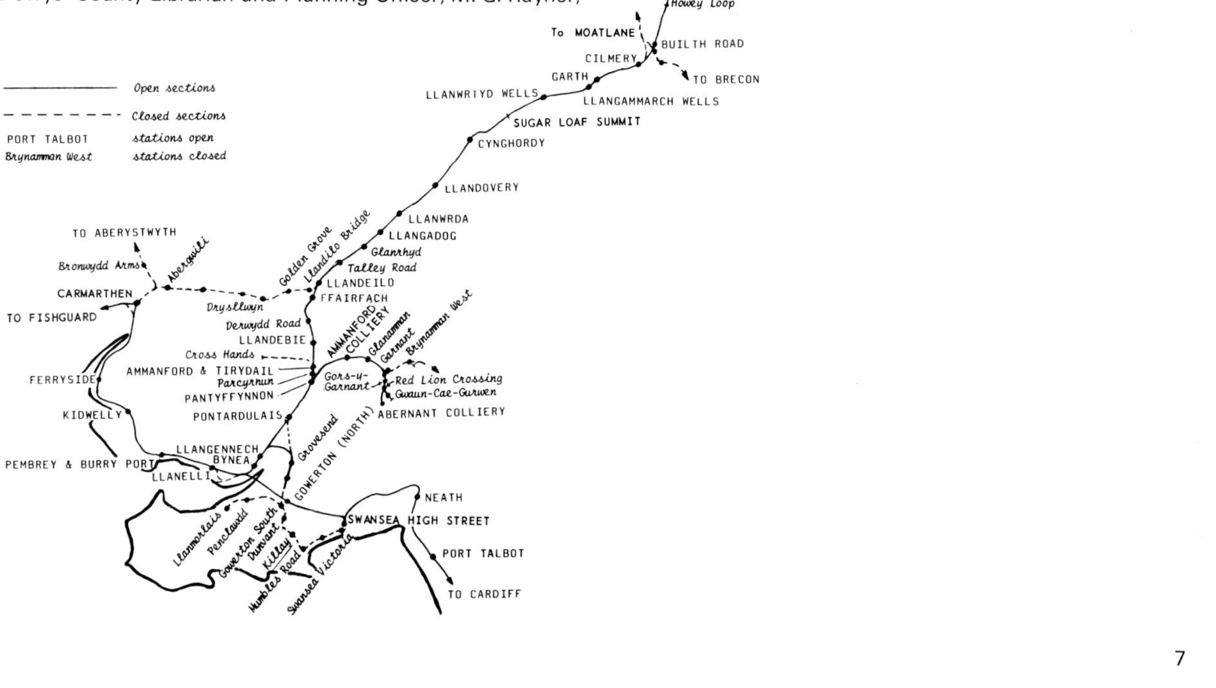

Above: Swansea Victoria was a terminus station with two platforms, engine release road and overall roof. Opened in 1882 to replace a wooden design of 1867, the trainshed suffered considerable damage thanks to the Luftwaffe. Tucked away from the main shopping area of the town it consequently had a somewhat neglected air about it. A GWR '57xx' pannier tank blasts out of the station with empty stock, watched by a startled shunter. In the other platform BR Standard Class 5 No 73036 awaits the departure time of 18.25 with the Swansea-York 'Mail'. *John White*

Left: The prewar condition of the overall roof is shown in this 1938 shot of Midland Johnson '1F' awaiting a shunt. Note the shunting pole strategically located in front of the smokebox. *H. C. Casserley*

Swansea Victoria-Pontardulais

Top right: Another prewar view showing LNWR Webb 0-6-2T No 7682 at the head of a local service for Pontardulais. These trains were operated under the push/pull system, with the locomotive remaining at the north end of the train for the southbound journey. *G. A. Hookham*

Centre right: March 1949 and an LNWR Webb 0-6-2T leaves Swansea Victoria with the 12.05 local to Pontardulais. This service was relatively intensive, running through the most densely populated section of the entire Central Wales route. *H. Daniel*

Right: In contrast to the locomotive shown in the previous picture, this LNWR Webb 2-4-2T is displaying the correct name of its owners. No 46620 stands by for its next local working on 20 April 1949. The engine is standing on a line which led behind the station, through a gateway and on to lines belonging to the Swansea Harbour Trust. *H. Daniel*

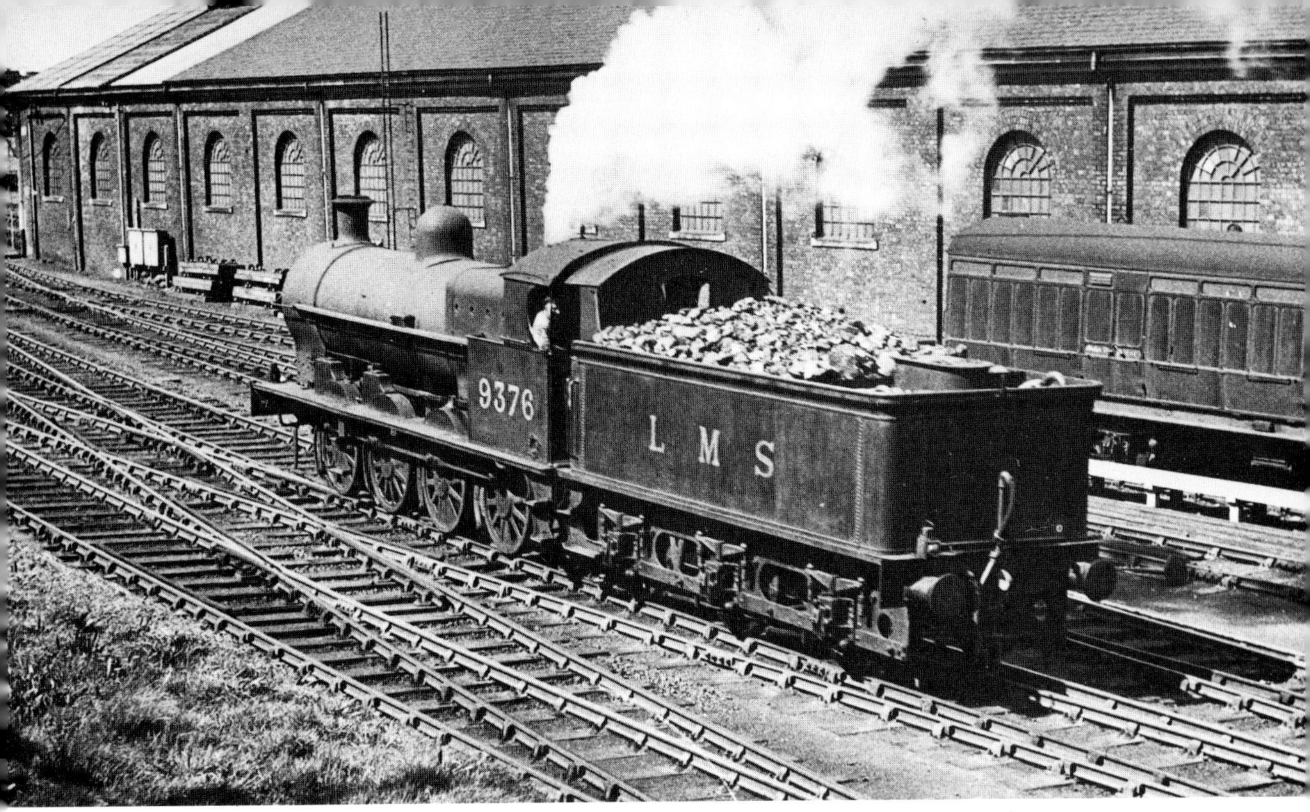

Above: Viewed from the embankment above the station, an LNWR Bowen Cooke 0-8-0 backs down towards the platform to remove and berth empty stock into the long carriage shed in the background. This dimly lit structure held stock overnight for the early morning departures. Certain 'ladies of the night' took advantage of this fact when plying their trade, to the horror of one particularly devout station master who frequently used to phone District Office in a terrible state on discovering such goings on. What exactly District Office were meant to do to solve the matter is not known! *H. Daniel*

Right: Behind the station was an elevated line which branched off the Central Wales route near No 1 Signalbox and ran across the town towards the North Dock and Eastern Depot on the other side of the River Tawe. There was also a branch off this line which emerged alongside the High Street station of the GWR. On 28 July 1957 a GWR pannier tank with 'Toad' brakevan attached passes above Swansea Victoria. *Hugh Davies*

Above: Power for trains on the route was provided (at the Swansea end) principally by Paxton Street shed (until its closure in 1959), located west of Swansea Victoria on the seaward side of the line. LNWR Bowen Cooke 0-8-0 No 8954 and LMS Stanier 'Black 5' No 5191 await events on 27 June 1938. The former class worked through freight services over the route for several decades, up to their withdrawal in the late 1950s. The 'Black 5s' were first seen on passenger working in 1936 and were a continuing presence until 1964.
H. C. Casserley

Right: With the carriage shed on the left and No 3 Signalbox in the background, the last passenger service before closure climbs the 1 in 45 bank out of the station. The locomotive is LMS Stanier 'Black 5' No 45406, the train is the 18.25 to York, and the date is 13 June 1964. With the closure of the 12 miles between Pontardulais and Swansea Victoria passenger trains were diverted to Llanelli and 'dieselised' (with the exception of summer Saturday services in that year). It is interesting to note that despite the terrain to be encountered by No 45406 it is seen here grappling with the steepest gradient on the whole route.
Gerald T. Robinson

Inset, left: Notwithstanding the continued use of the LNWR 0-8-0s on freight duties, the heaviest trains were usually allocated an LMS Stanier '8F'. Three are seen at Paxton Street shed on 27 August 1948. After closure of this depot its complement of engines was distributed to Llanelli, Swansea East Dock and Landore sheds, access being gained to the two latter shed by way of the cross town link via Wind Street viaduct. Unfortunately, this structure became unsafe in 1963, necessitating the changing of locomotives on down trains at Pantyffynnon, tank engines replacing the larger classes which could then gain access to the three sheds mentioned. *H. C. Casserley*

Below: On 18 April 1963 the 14.40 Shrewsbury-Swansea Victoria runs along the coast near Swansea Bay, hauled by a BR Standard 2-6-4T. These engines were introduced on the line in 1962, following their 'redundancy' caused by the electrification of the London-Tilbury-Southend route, and in effect, replaced the older LMS Fowler 2-6-4T design. *C. R. Berridge*

Above: On the same sunny evening one of 'Salop's' BR Standard Class 5s seen between the beach and the main road (and former trackbed of the Mumbles Railway) with the up 18.25 'York Mail' in the vicinity of Swansea Bay. Note the modern Mark 1 stock (complete with roofboard on the first vehicle). Between Swansea Victoria and Mumbles Road the prevailing wind blew sand from the beach on to the tracks, sufficient to warrant periodical engineers' trains to clean up.
C. R. Berridge

Centre right: Swansea Bay station in July 1955, with an LMS Stanier 2-6-2T heading a Craven Arms-Swansea train. Some members of this class made a brief visit to the line at this time, although their restricted fuel capacity no doubt made them unpopular with traincrews. Swansea Bay station had two signalboxes; whilst No 1 box was on the down platform, No 2 box was situated on the way to Victoria, controlling a level crossing and the entrance to a refuge siding.
Real Photographs

Right: LNWR Webb 2-4-2T No 46620 shrouds its front end in steam whilst standing at Mumbles Road station on 3 July 1950 with a Pontardulais bound local. The famous Mumbles Railway which operated between Swansea Rutland Street and Mumbles Pier had two physical connections with the Central Wales line; one was outside Swansea Victoria station which was a matter of yards from the tramway's Rutland Street terminus; the other was just beyond the underbridge visible in the background of this view of Mumbles Road. The bridge, in fact, crossed the main road and the Mumbles Railway. *G. A. Hookham*

Above: On the same day, with safety valves blowing, Stanier '8F' No 48478 coasts through Mumbles Road down platform with a local freight of miniscule proportions. During fine weather Mumbles Road was a highly popular destination for 'day trippers' from 'up line'. On Bank Holidays the up platform would be seething with folk making their way home after a day by the seaside.
G. A. Hookham

Centre left: From Mumbles Road the line turned inland, heading northwards through Clyne Woods, climbing at 1 in 70/80 before reaching Killay which is shown here looking south. The signalbox was closed in 1938 and replaced by a ground frame (released by Dunvant box) for gaining access to the sidings behind the down platform. There was also a siding from the down line, south of the station, which served the Clyne Valley Brickworks.
Lens of Sutton

Left: Dunvant station looking north. There were originally private sidings in both directions off both lines at the north end of the station. The buildings are of some interest in that they represent a standard design. The wooden shelter on the up platform and shed at the far end of the down platform in particular had several equals up the line. Indeed, a modified version of the latter remains as the shelter at Cynghordy. *Mowat Collection*

Left: A northbound passenger train behind a BR Standard Class 5 (in the 73090 series judging by the type of tender) leaves Dunvant in its wake. Few through trains called at all stations at the southern end of the line in view of the provision of a local service. *Ernest Morgan*

Below: Gowerton in August 1957 with an aged Webb 0-6-2T propelling its Pontardulais-Swansea local into the down platform. Originally (and more suitably) named Gower Road, the station became known as Gowerton South in 1886. Gowerton North is still open on the South Wales main line, and the remains of the bridge which took the Central Wales Line across the GWR route, north of the station, can still be seen at the west end of the surviving station, still served, of course, by trains to Central Wales and Shrewsbury (via Llanelli). *P. Ransome-Wallis*

Left: A general view of Gowerton looking north, showing the signalbox (beyond the footbridge) which controlled the facing junction from the up line to the Llanmorlais branch. Between Gowerton and Gorseinon was Glassbrooks signalbox from which ran sidings to a colliery and tinplate works. *Mowat Collection*

Above: A northbound 'local' is leaving Gorseinon seen from the footbridge on 11 July 1958. The chimneys on the left belonged to the Grovesend Steel Works. Practically nothing remains of either the station or the steel works, though Gorseinon still retains its rail connected coalyard. *H. C. Casserley*

Left: Only a week after this photograph was taken on 6 June 1964 Gorseinon station closed to passengers along with all others between Swansea Victoria and Pontardulais. Freight trips continued to run south of Gorseinon until 4 October 1965, and northwards to Pontardulais trips serving the coalyard at Gorseinon ran until 1974, when construction of the M4 necessitated closure of a section immediately south of Pontardulais. To overcome this problem a new spur was constructed at Grovesend Colliery Loop Junction trailing from the down Swansea District route (Court Sart Junction to Morlais Junction), rejoining the former Central Wales line near Brynlliw Colliery. *Roy Palmer*

Below left: Evidence of the old regime remains at Gorseinon in 1981. There is the amusing story of the stationmaster at Gorseinon who lived at neighbouring Gowerton and, when meeting passengers off an up train, charged his wife 'excess' for travelling with their child's pram without an additional ticket! The coalyard is served by a trip from Llanelli (Llandilo Junction yard). *Author*

Above: English Electric Type 3 diesels Nos 37.279 and 37.231 (photographed by their driver) stand at Brynlliw Colliery on the track which formerly constituted the down Central Wales line. The train is the '6086' — 04.00 Aberthaw to Brynlliw and return, whose 35 wagons are being loaded with coal for CEGB. When ready the train will proceed up 'the Central' and via the 1974 spur on to the Swansea District route at Grovesend Colliery Loop where the locos will runround before heading east. 4 June 1981 is the date.
R. W. Ranson

Left: Pontardulais station was situated in the 'V' between the diverging Swansea and Llanelli lines. Fowler 2-6-4T No 42385 arrives with the 14.40 Shrewsbury-Swansea train. The only track remaining today is that through the down Llanelli platform. The land used by the sidings in the left background has been occupied for several years by hundreds of allegedly defectively manufactured 'out of gauge' concrete sleepers. Not surprisingly, they cannot be found a suitable use, and are gradually disappearing behind the increasing undergrowth. *Lens of Sutton*

Left: GWR 0-6-2T No 5657 in the down Llanelli platform whilst in charge of a Stephenson Locomotive Society special in July 1955. Note the differing messages on the nameboards, relating to the two sets of platforms. *Real Photographs*

Above: In August 1957 Webb 0-6-2T No 58892 which has brought up a local from Swansea Victoria is crossing on to the down line (the bracket signal having been lowered) in order to set back in to the down platform. First stop on the return journey will be Gorseinon, although between 1910 and 1932 there was a halt at Grovesend near Brynlliw Colliery, two miles south of Pontardulais. *P. Ransome-Wallis*

Below: On the same day GWR 2-8-0 No 5209 rumbles through Pontardulais heading for Swansea Docks via Hendy Junction, the Swansea District line to Jersey Marine North Junction and Burrows Sidings. Export traffic still passes from Pantyffynnon via this route. *P. Ransome-Wallis*

Left: Between Pontardulais and Pantyffynnon the River Loughor is followed. Formerly double track this single line is now controlled by Port Talbot panel box, with Pantyffynnon being a 'fringe box'. During a misty February day in 1981 the 10.46 Shrewsbury-Swansea dmu passes 'downstream'. *Author*

Pontardulais-Llandovery

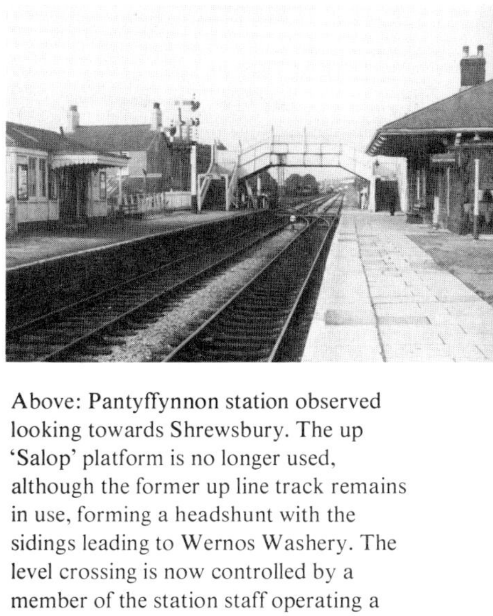

Above: Pantyffynnon station observed looking towards Shrewsbury. The up 'Salop' platform is no longer used, although the former up line track remains in use, forming a headshunt with the sidings leading to Wernos Washery. The level crossing is now controlled by a member of the station staff operating a ground frame at the far end of the down platform. The station building is currently used as a messroom, signing-on point for train crews, TOPS office, and supervisor's office. *John Stratton*

Left: The headshunt referred to above is seen on the right of the 10.46 Shrewsbury-Swansea five-car dmu as it heads south. Rather inconveniently, despite the presence of a signalbox, Pantyffynnon does not possess a passing loop on the Central Wales route. *BR*

The driver of the return local trip from Llandovery keeps a good look out as he sets back off the Central Wales line towards the sidings alongside the former Brynamman branch. The sidings leading to Wernos Washery can be seen in the background, above locomotive No 37.239. *BR*

Above: GWR 2-8-2T No 7232 underneath the coaling stage at Pantyffynnon shed which was constructed in 1931 and closed in September 1964. This locomotive class, along with the smaller '42xx' 2-8-0T species, worked the majority of the freight traffic originating from Pantyffynnon to Llanelli, Swansea Docks and eastwards. The shed was situated alongside the Brynamman branch. *D. M. Baldwin*

Above: The 14.58 Swansea-Shrewsbury two-car dmu passes the site of Parcyrhun Halt between Pantyffynnon and Ammanford & Tirydail. This halt was opened by the GWR in 1936 but closed 19 years later. The line north of Pantyffynnon as far as Llandrindod Wells was always single. Note the modern continuously welded track with Pandrol fittings, the only such section between Pantyffynnon and Craven Arms. *Author*

Above: Tirydail station was named Duffryn until 1889, and renamed Ammanford & Tirydail in 1960 following the closure of Ammanford station on the Brynamman line, and is now known simply as Ammanford/Rhydaman. Beyond the gates a branch veered left to Gulston Junction and Cross Hands, aptly known as the Mountain branch since it involved rope worked inclines at gradients as steep as 1 in 12. The signalbox shown here at the north end of the station remains in use (1982) to operate the level crossing. The present day passenger could be forgiven for being confused if travelling south in the rear vehicle since out of the platform-side window he will see a sign reading Ammanford, and out of the opposite window a sign on the signalbox wall reading Tirydail. In fact, there is a signalbox named Ammanford, but that is on the GCG branch from Pantyffynnon! *John Stratton*

Below: Llandebie, portrayed here in the early 1960s, looks not dissimilar today as it is one of the few unstaffed halts on the line where the buildings remain virtually unaltered. The main stone building is now used as the local Sheriff's office, whilst the signalbox has been retained to operate the level crossing. However, as at Tirydail, the crossing keeper has no signals to play with, protection for the gates being an elevated and illuminated stop board. Trains pass over the crossing upon receipt from the crossing keeper of a green handsignal waved from the box. Llandebie was unstaffed in 1965. *John Stratton*

Left: Although there were passing loops at Tirydail, Llandebie and Cilyrychen crossing, they could not deal with two conflicting passenger trains. The only location between Pantyffynnon and Llandilo where passenger trains could pass one another was here, at Derwydd Road, where the 07.45 Craven Arms-Swansea is waiting for the 'Jubilee' headed 10.25 Swansea-Shrewsbury to clear the single line. Trains from both directions have to climb towards Derwydd Road and it marks a watershed between the basins of the Loughor to the south, and Tywi/Towy to the north. *John Stratton*

Below left: As can be gleaned from this view of an up passenger train passing through the grassy platforms, Derwydd Road closed to passengers early in 1954, its signalbox and passing loop remaining until 1965. Approximately $\frac{2}{3}$-mile around the curve to the south is Cilyrychen crossing which still controls the passage of trains across the A438 road. From Cilyrychen a siding led from the up side to a nearby limestone quarry. *John Stratton*

Top right: From Derwydd Road the line falls through the twisting and sylvan valley of the River Cennen before reaching Ffairfach which retains its level crossing (now with lifting barriers and colour light signals) at the south end of the platform. The smaller stations south of Llandovery were not patronised by most of the through trains. Indeed, not so many years ago, a passenger at Llandrindod Wells (ex-LMS), wishing to travel to Ffairfach (ex-GWR) was shocked by a member of the station staff who genuinely denied all knowledge of the place! *Lens of Sutton*

Bottom right: BR Standard Class 4MT No 80133 passes through Ffairfach with a down train from Shrewsbury. Note the signalman offering up the token for the section to Derwydd Road. The small bracket signal was provided to gain access in to the milk depot on the east side of the line. *John Stratton*

Above: After crossing the River Towy northbound trains run into Llandilo station which was the terminus for trains from Carmarthen. This view shows both up and down main line platforms and the Carmarthen Bay platform on the down side. The town itself is perched on the side of a hill to the left of the photograph. Once the through route was opened, the platforms were lengthened, the new section being higher than the original, thus necessitating a slope on the up side underneath the footbridge. *Lens of Sutton*

Below: On 16 May 1964 a Stanier 'Black 5' stands in the down platform waiting the road. A new brick signalbox was built in 1955 to replace the three former boxes (one at each end of the station and one at Carmarthen Valley Junction). The Carmarthen branch veered westwards after sharing the bridge crossing the river. *A. M. Watson collection*

Above: This view, taken from above Llandilo station, gives a good impression of the topography the railway accompanies between Llandilo and Llandovery. It is a common sight from the train to see fishermen wading into the Towy, and a footpath crosses the river near the south end of the bay platform on suspension bridge. Another 'picturesque' feature is the 'Refreshment Room' which is still in use on the up platform (in effect as a privately owned public house). *D. J. Clarke Collection*

Left: North of Llandilo, on the former Vale of Towy Railway (which opened to Llandovery in 1858) is a long straight which passes through the former stations of Talley Road and Glanrhyd (the latter being shown here). Both were served only by local trains and were closed in 1955. Only the station house remains at Talley Road, the village of Talley being over seven miles away to the west. At Glanrhyd the station building is still occupied, its front door opening on to the platform. Stanier '8F' No 48308 hurries north with a passenger train for Shrewsbury on 18 July 1953. *G. A. Hookham*

Bottom left: A fatal accident took place at the level crossing situated at the north end of the platform when, on 7 March 1959, Stanier 'Black 5' No 45283, hauling the up 'York Mail', doubtless at some speed, hit a car which was being mistakenly driven across the line. Today the now ungated level crossing is subject to a 25mph speed restriction (which rather spoils a fast run) despite the fact that the lane concerned is little more than a muddy track simply leading to the river bank. Glanrhyd is seen here on 29 December 1980. *Author*

Above: In contrast to other similar routes (notably the Cambrian Coast line) there is no longer any schools traffic on the Central Wales line. Formerly, a service for schoolchildren operated from Llandovery to Llangadog, where a Stanier '8F' is about to run round its enormous load prior to returning 'empty stock' to Llandovery. Having completed this easy task the engine would find more strenuous work banking trains from Llandovery up to Sugar Loaf summit. *John Stratton*

Left: The impressive stone building on the up platform at Llangadog (spelt Llangadock until 1958) gave the station an air of importance. Here and at Llanwrda were the only passing loops on the 11 miles between Llandeilo and Llandovery. At the south end of Llangadog there was a private siding which diverged from the up line to serve the creamery (adjacent to which is a sewage works!) *John Stratton*

Bottom left: Llanwrda station had the unusual feature of staggered platforms. 'Jubilee' class No 45572 runs southwards into the former up platform with a passenger train in the summer of 1964. Before Nationalisation in 1948 the Llandilo-Llandovery section was jointly owned by the LMS and GWR. The line north of Llangadog was maintained by the LMS and south of Llangadog by the GWR; note, therefore, the contrasting styles of architecture used at Llangadog and Llanwrda. *David Mathew*

Left: Local farmers used the railway to shift their possessions by hiring a farm removal train. GWR 'Dean Goods' No 2382 stands in the down platform waiting to move the agricultural contents from Llanwrda to 'pastures new' on 2 October 1934. In the Vale of Towy the railway passes through a relatively prosperous farming area and local freight traffic levels reflected this fact. *BR*

Below: The modern scene at Llanwrda. The now standard wooden shelter offers no passengers to the 10.46 Shrewsbury-Swansea dmu which is passing over the ungated level crossing at a theoretical 10mph. As can be seen, up trains have to be even more cautious. *H. J. Ashman/BR*

Above: Following another long straight north of Llanwrda a left hand bend leads on to Llwynjack Bridge (across the Towy for the last time). Fowler Class 4 No 42305 takes this curve heading south with the 07.40 Craven Arms-Swansea on 30 April 1956. At one time the Craven Arms guard who worked this train returned north from Swansea with the 12.25 to Shrewsbury (as far as Craven Arms). Subsequently this diagram was altered so that the guard worked the 07.40 down as far as Llanwrtyd, returning north with the 07.45 Swansea as far as Shrewsbury, and finally booking off at Craven Arms after working down the 12.00 Shrewsbury to Swansea. The driver and fireman off the 07.40 used to swap footplates with Llandovery men on the up local goods. *G. A. Hookham*

Left: Stanier Class 3 Tank No 40141 crosses Llwynjack Bridge with the 12.00 Shrewsbury-Swansea on 12 August 1955 during this type of locomotive's brief workout on the line. The meandering river is never far away from the railway in the Vale of Towy and, consequently, this section represents the straightest and flattest part of the route, encouraging relatively high speeds from the more 'enterprising' drivers. *C. J. Sarah*

Above: A posed general view of Llandovery, which once boasted two motive power depots and a Control Office. The GWR shed was a one road structure behind the up platform (on the left of the photograph). The station itself was always busy serving, as it does, a market town with quite a considerable rural catchment area. *Lens of Sutton*

Left: The LNWR/LMS loco shed at Llandovery was necessarily much larger than that of the GWR. Whilst GWR engines were used on the local services that ran down sedately to Llanelli, the LNWR/LMS had to provide resources for passenger and freight workings northwards over the hills, therefore needing more (and larger) locomotives. The shed also possessed a 42ft turntable (to the immediate right of the photographer). Closure took place in 1964. Needless to say the depot had its quota of characters; 'the Flying Finn' and 'Captain Sparks', for example, or the driver who kept pigs and was also fond of beer; whilst his 'Missis' was away for a few days he killed one of the pigs and sold it for 'pop money'. Knowing what his wife's reaction would have been to such a scheme, he built a mound of earth in his back yard, and told her that one of the litter had sadly died due to natural causes during her absence. *John Stratton*

Left: Involved in shunting duties, an LNWR 'Cauliflower' goods is seen here in August 1939, berthing livestock wagons in the cattlepen siding at the south end of Llandovery station. *G. A. Hookham*

Centre left: Another venerable locomotive of LNWR design — 0-8-4T No 7941 stands in the up platform at Llandovery. This engine was allocated to banking freight trains (or piloting overloaded passenger trains) up the incline to Sugar Loaf summit. It also worked the daily local goods train to Craven Arms and on at least one occasion replaced a failed Fowler 2-6-4T on the 18.05 local passenger to Craven Arms. *G. A. Hookham*

Bottom left: More conventional passenger power; a Fowler 2-6-4T of the later build, with riveted side tanks, compared to the smoother sides found on the earlier numbers. The loco has probably just taken water, and will have to refill at both Builth Road and Knighton, much to the annoyance of the fireman. The climb from Llandovery to Sugar Loaf summit is $8\frac{1}{2}$ miles, steepening before Cynghordy to 1 in 60, so the fireman had to obtain a healthy boiler pressure before setting out from Llandovery. *G. A. Hookham*

Top right: The Llandovery North signalman improvises in handing the single line token to the crew of this Shrewsbury bound train. No 75000, the first BR Standard Class 4 4-6-0 to be constructed, was only two years old when seen here on 17 July 1953. These locomotives were only used for a short time on the Central Wales line following their introduction. However, their larger brothers, the Class 5 of the '73xxx' series, became staple passenger power along with Stanier 'Black 5s' and Fowler 2-6-4Ts on through services during the 1950s and early 1960s.
G. A. Hookham

Bottom right: The local service between Llandovery and Llanelli was usually worked by GWR pannier tanks, but '56xx' 0-6-2Ts were also used occasionally. On 17 July 1953 a pannier tank of the '57xx' class enters the down platform at Llandovery with two empty coaches after propelling out and crossing over from the up platform. *G. A. Hookham*

75000

3771

Llandovery-Llandrindod

Not surprisingly there was (and still is) great rivalry between the LNWR/LMS and GWR factions on the route. Supporters of the former north of Llandovery used to mock the arrival of the train photographed here climbing the initial 1 in 87 bank out of Llandovery behind a '57xx' class pannier tank on 8 July 1950. This represented the only regular passenger working by GWR locomotives north of Llandovery, it being the summer Saturdays 08.20 Llanelli to Llandrindod Wells (which returned south at 13.15). This train terminated at Llandovery during the week, but was extended on summer Saturdays during the 1950s. Note the removal of the engine's steam heating pipe from beneath the buffer beam. *G. A. Hookham*

Left: Approximately ¾-mile further up the line from the last photograph the 10.25 Swansea-Shrewsbury is seen on 18 July 1953, hauled by the unusual combination of GWR 0-6-2T No 5675 piloting BR Standard Class 4 No 75000. This implies that the train engine, No 75000 was not rated by its crew, since this type was permitted to take 200 tons unassisted up the bank to Sugar Loaf summit, a figure just sufficient to allow for the six coaches being hauled on this occasion. It is interesting to compare this load restriction figure for the 1 in 60 ruling gradient with the 288 tons (and later 300 tons) allowed for the same class of engine up the 1 in 52 gradient of Talerddig bank on the Cambrian route. *G. A. Hookham*

Left: Cynghordy on the same day, with an LNWR 0-8-0 about to pass through the platform, hauling an up freight with the brickworks chimney in the background — the only industrial site for many a mile! For the first 3¾ miles out of Llandovery the climb varies from between 1 in 80 to 1 in 200, and the track is well aligned. However, from a point about 1 mile below Cynghordy the gradient steepens to 1 in 60, and the line becomes more curved. *G. A. Hookham*

Below: During the 1981 nationwide tour of the prototype Class 140 dmu the unit made a demonstration run from Carmarthen to Cynghordy and back on 30 June. The unit is seen here returning south past the former station house at Cynghordy. The unit returned for a trial period on the line in January 1982 but failed to operate certain track circuits. Following modification it continued its trial in the following June. *James McGregor*

Above: The occupants of the brakevan's rear verandah are clearly more interested in having their picture taken than sheltering inside from the undoubted din coming from the chimney of GWR 0-6-2T No 5675 as it 'assists in rear' a freight through Cynghordy. *G. A. Hookham*

Below: With less noise a BR Standard 2-6-4T on 22 May 1964 comes to a stand at Cynghordy with the 11.45 Shrewsbury-Swansea. The station had only one platform, the passing loop and runaway siding being installed in 1929. Consequently it was impossible to cross two stopping passenger trains here, although this did not present a real problem since more passenger trains passed than stopped! *W. G. Sumner*

Right: Stanier '8F' No 48444 with the up local freight to Craven Arms approaches Cynghordy viaduct, north of the station. Note the tidy condition of the trackside walking path, or 'cess' as it is known, and the visual difference between the metal and wooden keys which hold the bullhead rail in place. Central Wales track, especially between Llandovery and Craven Arms, was always immaculately maintained. The wire seen running beside the track controlled Cynghordy down distant signal, which was situated north of the viaduct. *IAL*

Above: A Shrewsbury bound dmu grinds over Cynghordy viaduct at a steady 39mph, if in decent condition and not having stopped at the station. The viaduct has 18 arches, is 283yd long, up to 102ft high and is on a 26 chain curve. Chiefly of stone, the arches are lined in brick. *Sid Morris*

Right: The 10.46 Salop-Swansea, formed of a Swindon built two-car set and a Gloucester built three-car unit, passes over Cynghordy viaduct on Saturday 15 August 1981. Despite the more modern form of traction, the most common location for failures is still the section climbing to Sugar Loaf. Whereas, prior to 1964 help could be sought from Llandovery, assistance now has to come from Pantyffynnon (or even Llanelli). On one Sunday a return Llandrindod Wells-Newport dmu excursion failed at one end of the viaduct. There being no resources at Pantyffynnon, a light engine eventually made its way from Llanelli to rescue the dmu, whose passengers at least had the consolation of a wonderful view during their wait! *Author*

Below right: Viewed from over $\frac{3}{4}$-mile away on the main A483 road, a ballast train hauled by shunters Nos 03.145 and 03.151 struggles across Cynghordy viaduct on Sunday 16 August 1981. There is a local legend that the bridge is haunted due to the death of one of the contractor's staff during the building of the seventh pier. *Author*

Above: One of Shrewsbury's BR Standard Class 5s approaches the viaduct heading south with the 11.45 Shrewsbury-Swansea on 11 October 1962. An LNWR 0-8-0 descending from Sugar Loaf ran out of control with a freight carrying pig iron in 1936. The train overran the sand drag and the driver died from his injuries. *IAL*

Left: Nos 03.145 and 03.151 make their way slowly up the 1 in 60 grade towards Sugar Loaf. These locos are driven in multiple, being connected by numerous control gear leads between the cabs, which therefore have to be marshalled 'back to back'. *Author*

Left: BR Standard Class 5 No 73091 pollutes the rarified atmosphere as it heads towards the dismally damp 1,000yd Sugar Loaf tunnel. A stream runs across the top of the tunnel and is chiefly responsible for the constant cascade through the roof, especially nearer the northern portal. Trainmen in difficulties were instructed to stop for a 'blow up' outside rather than inside the tunnel, in view of its unpleasant conditions.
Anthony A. Vickers

Below left: The final climb towards Sugar Loaf tunnel is scenically one of the most spectacular few miles of BR. The railway can be viewed from high up across the valley on the actual Sugar Loaf mountain, low cloud, rain and mist permitting. From this point it is possible to follow the progress of an up train from almost Cynghordy viaduct along the hillside ledge and in to the tunnel. During the late 1950s the slopes beneath the track were planted by the Forestry Commission and the growth of these trees has impaired the views of and from the railway. The hill above these toiling Stanier '8Fs' and their freight is called Bryn Nichol.
John Stratton

Top right: A down passenger with a Stanier 'Black 5' at its head passes the summit, the fireman and signalman preparing to exchange tokens, on 25 May 1959. During the winter of 1949/50 the line through the tunnel was closed for eight weeks when loose keystones in the roof were discovered. Since the navvies started its construction the tunnel has always been a source of trouble to the engineers. Beyond the signalbox can be seen a circular sign with a diagonal band, indicating the termination of a section of route through a Forestry Plantation.
D. Fish

Bottom right: On 24 March 1961 the noon Shrewsbury-Swansea passenger pulled by BR Standard Class 5 No 73090 passes the summit. The houses (since demolished) above the box were inhabited by members of staff, and the short platforms were for their use in reaching 'civilisation'. This particular train was booked to call for the purpose of picking up or setting down staff and their dependents if required.
Anthony A. Vickers

SUGAR LOAF SUMMIT
44835

SUGAR LOAF SUMMIT
73090

Left: The gradient climbing from the Llandovery direction changes from 1 in 80 to 1 in 70 outside the southern portal of the tunnel. At 820ft above sea level, Sugar Loaf summit is still 160ft below the peak of the line at Llangunllo. The track falling towards Llanwrtyd Wells passes over Berthddu level crossing (where the deafness of one of the crossing keepers often caused the adjacent signalmen anxiety) and crosses marshy terrain allegedly 'soaked up' by absorbent layers of sheep's wool underneath the ballast.
John Stratton

Right: Llanwrtyd Wells, where one can still 'take the waters'. The 10.25 Swansea-Manchester arrives on a Saturday in high summer, powered by Fowler 2-6-4T No 42385. This train would have been preceded by a 10.15 Swansea-Shrewsbury relief, and would be followed by the 09.30 Pembroke Dock-Shrewsbury. The railway, of course, caused the development of the Central Wales Spa towns. The remaining derelict spring at Llanwrtyd is about half a mile from the village which, itself, is half a mile west of the station. It is worth the walk, however, for even on the hottest day the sulphur water is ice cool as it bubbles up from beneath the ground. It smells of rotten eggs, but is devoid of a similar taste. It is said to purify the blood, and is recommended for curing hangovers!
Ernest Morgan

Above left: In August 1939 the Saturdays Only extension of a Llanelli-Llandovery local to Llanwrtyd prepares to return south behind GWR '57xx' class pannier No 7755. Llanwrtyd remains the most photogenic station on the line, though changes since 1965 have included the shortening of the up platform and removal of the footbridge, goods yard sidings, downside platform buildings and water columns. *G. A. Hookham*

Above right: In 1967, in an attempt to reduce double-heading on the Pantyffynnon-Gwaun-cae-Gurwen/Abernant coal trains, the original series of North British Locomotive Co, 'Warship' class diesels was transferred from Plymouth to Pantyffynnon. No D602 *Bulldog* made a test run to Llandrindod Wells on 22 August 1967, and is seen here at Llanwrtyd with a posse of inspectors in the cab and Relief Signalman Jim Smout on the platform. For a few months these engines worked the local Pantyffynnon-Llandrindod freight, though their stay on the line was shortlived as the experiment on the Pantyffynnon branches was not a success. *Ernest Morgan*

Below: Llanwrtyd retains its passing loop which is booked to cross the day's last two passenger trains. The tail lamp of the 18.46 ex-Shrewsbury contrasts with the marker lights of the 18.50 ex-Swansea, which is still known as 'the Mail'. Traincrews are exchanged at this evening ritual, and tea is usually made prior to the respective departures. For this Shrewsbury crew Llanwrtyd is the only staffed station, other than Shrewsbury, that they encounter. In fact, the guard does one return trip to Llandrindod Wells crossing, followed by the return trip to Llanwrtyd — 238½ miles and 54 potential unstaffed station stops! Both Swindon Cross Country dmus shown here are three-car, rather than the usual two-car formation, so both drivers will have to 'use their initiative' in order to arrive home on time. *Sid Morris*

Above: No 47151 seen from the top of Llanwrtyd Wells down distant signal on 28 April 1979 with a York-Llanwrtyd Wells weekend excursion. At Shrewsbury an attempt was made to fit the newly introduced portable spotlight. Unfortunately, standardisation on BR being what it is, the plug on the lead and the socket in the cab were incompatible so the driver put his bardic handlamp on the front instead. Portable headlamps are also available now for attaching to dmus. *Author*

Centre right: Whilst the line descends through the Irfon Valley from Sugar Loaf summit to the Wye bridge at Builth Road, there are uphill starts for northbound trains from both Llangammarch Wells and Garth stations. The single platform building at Llangammarch was of shiny red brick, formerly backed by a siding.
Powys County Information Service/Ann Morris

Bottom right: Until recently a common sight in the van of a Central Wales passenger train was pigeon baskets. At a nominated station (in this case Llangammarch Wells) a member of the station staff would release the birds which hopefully would find their way home to lofts at the south end of the line. The time of release would be noted on a label attached to the basket which was then returned empty on the next down train. An originating traffic from Llangammarch before World War 2 was crates full of bottles containing barium water. There were consigned to the ailing middle and upper classes of London, who could continue a course of the waters which would have commenced, no doubt, with a fortnight's stay at the Lake Hotel. Most spa waters lose their healing properties if not consumed quickly, but barium water retains its potency and therefore was suitable for transportation. *Ernest Morgan*

Above: After climbing out of Llangammarch and passing through a short tunnel, the line falls towards Garth, crossing the river Irfon twice. The last 12.25 Swansea-Shrewsbury of 1979 approaches Garth, formed by Swindon built power cars Nos W50722 and W50672, which until 1982 worked on the line almost continuously (barring downtime for maintenance and shopping) from June 1964. The train is manned by a Shropshire crew who work the 10.46 from Shrewsbury as far as Llandilo, where they change over with the Swansea men on the 12.25 ex-Swansea. As there is no time for a half hour 'physical needs break' between the third and fifth hour of their diagram, the turn is double-manned. *Author*

Left: The main building at Garth was on the upside, being of a unique design. It looked more like a cottage than a station, with its dumpy appearance and end wall (facing the prevailing wind) protected by slates suspended from wooden latticework — this architectural feature being common in Central Wales. The buildings at Garth and Llangammarch were demolished in 1980. *Powys County Information Service/Ann Morris*

Above: The downside at Garth had only a wooden shelter (of 1871 vintage) identical to those found at several other stations on the line. Garth was the only crossing station between Llanwrtyd and Builth Road until the box was closed in 1965. *John Stratton*

Below: With railway cottages in the background, the fireman of a down passenger train changes tokens with Signalman Gareth Bevan at Garth. The BR Standard Class 5 shown was one of a small number of regular performers on the route. A feature of the provision of power on the line has always been the persistent use, over a number of years, of a few individual engines. *Ernest Morgan*

Above: This lower quadrant ground signal of LNWR origin controlled the entrance to the goods yard, which was situated on the upside, south of the station. A signalbox of Midland design was erected in 1933 (to replace an earlier structure) which was similar to those built at Cynghordy in 1929 and Hopton Heath in 1945. The lever frame was 'the wrong way round', facing the rear wall of the box rather than the track. *John Stratton*

Above: Somewhat like the Somerset & Dorset line, when loads were heavier on summer Saturdays, freight engines were put to use on passenger trains over the route, to save additional piloting costs. Theoretically limited to 50mph the Stanier '8Fs' were a common sight on such workings as this down train at Garth on 13 September 1959. This class of engine was permitted to haul 300 tons unassisted when working passenger trains. *G. A. Hookham*

Left: The section between Garth and Cilmery is punctuated by several short straights separated by reverse curves, and is paralleled by the A483 road. Occasionally, drivers of up trains have been known to lose their exact bearings as a result of this repetitive pattern, braking too soon for Cilmery station! However, the driver of this freight train has no problem as he is heading south and has Garth distant signal to act as a landmark. The ex-LMS faction among the traincrew establishment often light-heartedly accuse the 'Western' men of not knowing where they are when driving over the more remote sections of the route. *Anthony A. Vickers*

Left: Cilmery, with a locomotive combination of interest passing through on a Llanelli-Blackpool excursion (for the illuminations) on 25 October 1975. This was the one and only time that a Class 47 diesel (No 47.252) was piloted by a Class 37 (No 37.177) over the line, providing the most powerful diesel combination ever seen on a passenger train. Cilmery had a couple of sidings on the up side of the line, to the south of the station, until 1959. It is overlooked by Llywelyn's Monument which marks where the last 'native' Prince of Wales met his end in 1282. *David Rowe*

Right: A general view of the south end of the Builth Road High Level (as it was named). In the foreground is the bridge over the Mid Wales route, whilst behind the two sided signal post can be seen the small engine shed which housed the locomotive used for shunting and banking duties. The Cambrian line had its local motive power depot at Builth Wells, $1\frac{1}{2}$ miles away towards Brecon. *John Stratton*

Above: Builth Road was a railway crossroads, the Central Wales line crossing over the Cambrian Mid Wales line from Brecon to Moat Lane Junction. There was a physical rail connection between the two routes by way of a line leading from the up side of the LNWR line northwards, to trail into the Cambrian line. This spur was not regularly used by through freight or passenger trains, but did see the occasional special working; on 20 July 1904 a Royal Train conveying Edward VII and Queen Alexandra travelled from Swansea Victoria to the Elan Valley reservoirs near Rhayader via this link, on the day of the dams' official opening. The spur was also used by a Barry-Llandrindod Wells Saturday working which ran during the summer of certain inter-war years. In order to shunt sidings towards the lower level, a Stanier '8F' takes the left turn off the Central Wales route whilst working the Llandovery-Craven Arms 'local' pickup freight. *John Stratton*

Right: A Swansea based Fowler 2-6-4T working home with the 14.40 Shrewsbury-Swansea train stands at Builth Road in August 1960. The platforms were linked by a subway and the two stations by a path and luggage lift. Being a 'railway centre' a settlement quickly evolved with the arrival of the railway. The several rows of brick terraced houses of a design seen on all parts of the former LNWR system, remain today as a reminder of the village's 'raison d'etre'. The substantial building on the down platform is now converted into flats. As well as the engine shed, there was an engineering depot, forge and workshop (alongside the spur) which are now within a timber yard. *C. Smith*

50

42394

Above: In July 1957 one of the regular Stanier 'Black 5s' arrives with an up passenger. Nos 44835, 45143, 45145, 45190, 45283, 45298 (with a self-weighing tender) and 45406 were commonly used members of this famous class. Builth Road possessed a bay platform on the up side used by the occasional local trains which were part of the service until the 1960s. *Real Photographs*

Centre left: The 11.45 Shrewsbury-Swansea with BR Standard Class 5 No 73090 heads south across the by then closed Brecon-Moat Lane line on 10 June 1964. In the background, beyond the front of the locomotive, can be seen the spur line's junction with the Mid Wales route. An engineering train recovering the Cambrian line is standing in the up platform of the Low Level station. The Refreshment Room on the other platform remains in used as a Public House. *B. J. Ashworth*

Bottom left: Most up freights were banked up the 1 in 74 gradient from Builth Road to Howey Loop. From the crossing of the River Wye half a mile south of the station, the line climbs towards the Ithon Valley. Today it is difficult to comprehend how intensively the route was used by through freight trains. Most of the signalboxes were open continuously throughout three shifts and, as late as 1961, 10 through freights trains each way took this way to and from such yards as Coton Hill and Coleham (Shrewsbury), Crewe, Burton-on-Trent, Stafford, Saltney (Chester), Swansea Eastern Depot, Llandilo Junction (Llanelli) and Pontardulais. Stanier '8F' No 48463 apparently did not require help on this occasion and sets out northwards from Builth Road. *Ernest Morgan*

Right: Howey Passing Loop marked the end of the 1 in 74 climb out of the Wye Valley. The loop was opened in 1912 and lasted 50 years. Banking locos were usually dropped off at this point, although some of the heaviest freights were booked for assistance between Builth Road and Llangunllo — a distance of 19 miles. Banking engines returning to their base would often be coupled to suitably timed freight trains or other light engine movements to save finding them an additional path. A down freight is seen here cautiously passing through the loop.
John Stratton

Below: Howey village is to the north of the former passing loop and, being quite sizeable, it is surprising that the provision of a halt to serve the community progressed no further than the discussion stage. Part of the problem was that no one could agree exactly where to locate the station as the 'built up area' stretches, ribbon-like, for 1¼ miles, parallel to the railway and A483 road. One possible site is being passed by Stanier 'Jubilee' class *Bengal* with the 09.45 Swansea-Shrewsbury on 10 June 1964. If, when waiting on Llandrindod station one can hear an up train passing through Howey, this indicates a south-westerly wind and is a fairly reliable predictor of impending rain.
B. J. Ashworth

Left: Prior to the coming of the railway in 1865, the postal address of Llandrindod Wells was 'near Howey, Radnorshire'. The railway transformed Llandrindod into a town and fashionable spa. Consequently, Howey is now 'near Llandrindod Wells'. In the spa's heyday trains were met by fleets of porters with handcarts, ready to convey passengers' luggage to the numerous hotels. Two LNWR stalwarts, a 2-4-0 piloting a 4-6-2 'Prince of Wales' tank, arrive at Llandrindod with their pre-World War 1 express for Shrewsbury. The line doubled at Llandrindod station until 1958, when the station signalbox on the down platform (to the left of the signalman shown) was closed and the up platform taken out of use. This decision has caused considerable inconvenience to countless passengers on down trains wishing to end their journey at Llandrindod who have to wait, when up trains run late, at the remaining signalbox $\frac{3}{4}$-mile north of the station. The north end of the town is known as 'the Crossing', named after the level crossing controlled by the signalbox. *A. M. Watson Collection*

Centre left: From 15 June 1964 Central Wales line passenger services to and from Shrewsbury were diverted to Llanelli upon closure of the Swansea Victoria-Pontardulais section. Also at this time, dmus replaced steam power on all trains, with the exception of the Saturday services during the remainder of that summer, which continued to be steam hauled. In August of 1964, Salop based BR Standard Class 5 No 73097 awaits the 'right away' from Llandrindod, with a train for Llanelli. There was a sizeable goods yard on the down side between the level crossing and the station. A narrow gauge line serving a nearby quarry ended above the goods yard on a wooden viaduct used for overhead discharge into wagons beneath. This operation ceased when the viaduct burnt down. *Roy Palmer*

Bottom left: In the early 1960s the disused up platform at 'Llandod' (as it is known to the locals) was used to store much of the equipment for the proposed Centralised Traffic Control Scheme which entailed the construction of a new signalbox at Llandrindod to operate in its entirety the line between Llandovery and Craven Arms (which would have been continuously track circuited). The aim was to improve line capacity for the then projected increases in freight traffic for the route, whilst also leading to savings brought about by the closure of 18 signalboxes and conversion of level crossings to automatic half barrier status. The scheme was approved by the British Transport Commission in 1960, at a cost of £676,000 but, unfortunately, this decision was subsequently reversed and the equipment lay rusting on site for over two years. It is interesting to speculate how the present role of the line might have differed had the CTC project been implemented. The up platform building is now used as the line's headquarters of the permanent way department. *M. Walters*

Above: Llandrindod station has the distinction of being Queen Elizabeth II's first Welsh 'landfall' following her accession to the throne. On 23 October 1952, when the Queen opened the Claerwen Dam in the Elan Valley complex, the Royal Train arrived in Llandrindod at 10.15, having left Paddington at 22.30 the previous night, with an overnight stop between 03.50 and 08.55, hidden away at Marsh Farm Junction on the truncated remains of the Craven Arms-Much Wenlock line. The stock remained at Llandrindod for the 17.30 return journey, whilst the train engines were sent to Llandovery for servicing and turning. Needless to say, the station was suitably spruced up for the occasion, after which a commemorative stone was laid in the platform to mark the exact spot where the Queen first stepped on to Welsh ground. *BR*

Below: To the utter horror and disgust of the LMS faction, two 'Castle' class locomotives of GWR design were chosen to head the 11-coach Royal Train throughout — even on to the Central Wales line. The two years old No 7030 *Cranbrook Castle* and No 7036 *Taunton Castle* were the selected engines, whilst another ex-GWR locomotive, No 6971 *Athelhampton Hall* ran down from Craven Arms in front of the Royal Train and shunted the empty stock at Llandrindod. Nos 7030 and 7036 are seen here approaching Llandrindod's crossing box. GWR 4-6-0 designs never worked regularly over the route, even after the line passed into Western Region control. This was due, it is said, to clearance problems between Pantyffynnon and Llandovery. *BR*

Left: On the up platform at Penybont can be seen four concrete flower holders inscribed 'Safety', 'Speed', 'Comfort' and 'Efficiency'. Between the two central pillars a rhyme is written into the concrete floor:

'The kiss of the sun for a pardon,
The song of the birds for mirth,
One is nearer God's heart in a garden
Than anywhere else on earth'.

The gardens at Penybont were renowned for their high standard, and were decorated by thousands of tiny sea shells. *Author*

Llandrindod-Knighton

Left: Between Llandrindod and Penybont the line was double until 1965. The 'up local' freight has climbed the 1 in 74 bank from the Ithon bridge through the village of Crossgates and is awaiting shunting instructions at Penybont. The railway passes approximately 1¼ miles from Penybont village, whilst Crossgates, though adjacent to the line is unserved. In 1970 a local referendum was held with a view to moving the station to Crossgates. Of those who bothered to vote, 64 were in favour and 48 against. In view of this unclear majority the idea was abandoned by the working party of local interests set up to liaise with BR on matters of mutual interest following the second reprieve of the line in 1969. *Derek Cross*

Below left: At the north end of Penybont station the line singled to pass through the straight 404yd long Penybont tunnel, climbing again at 1 in 74 to Penybont Junction signalbox where the line doubled. The up distant signal for Penybont Junction can be seen at the north end of the up platform in this photograph of BR Standard Class 5 No 73035 leaving Penybont with a heavy summer Saturday down train of seven coaches. The engine, being based at Shrewsbury, has an 89A shedplate and also has a self cleaning (SC) smokebox. It is interesting to note the changing codes over the years for Shrewsbury shed, as witnessed by the 84G, 89A and 6D seen on the front of Salop based locomotives included in this book. *W. A. Camwell*

Below right: Penybont Junction was never a junction in the proper sense; it simply represented the north end of the short bottleneck section through the tunnel. There was once a scheme to extend the Leominster-New Radnor branch over Radnor Forest to cross the Central Wales line at this point, before continuing towards Rhayader and Aberystwyth. The double track between Penybont Junction and Llanbister Road was singled in 1964, and this led to the closure of the former box. The white board attached to the corner of the box was provided to assist drivers' sighting of the up home signal which was situated in the deep rock cutting north of the tunnel. The down line had already been taken out of use when this Stanier '8F' passed the then closed signalbox in 1964, with a freight for Llandilo Junction. *John Stratton*

Below: Taken from the same viewpoint as the previous photograph 15 years later, the 10.46 Shrewsbury-Swansea passes the site of Penybont Junction. There were six Swindon two-car Cross Country units fitted with spotlights for use over the route (numbered C600 to C605) which were later supplemented by four three-car sets (numbered C610-C613) which, in 1980, were replaced by five sets (C615, C616, C620, C621 and C622) transferred from Inverness. From May 1982 less comfortable Metro Cammell units from Bristol replaced the Swindon sets (some of which had spent almost 18 years on the line). *Author*

Right: Dolau station is situated on a $2\frac{1}{2}$-mile straight in the broad valley of the River Aran (a tributary of the River Ithon), overlooked to the east by the Radnor Forest massif (which is, in fact, largely treeless). On a miserable, grey day in 1964 the 14.40 Shrewsbury-Swansea arrives at Dolau. The locomotive is a BR Standard Class 4 tank No 80097. *John Stratton*

Bottom right: From the same viewpoint the 14.58 Swansea-Shrewsbury on 14 February 1981 about to cross the roadway north of Dolau station. The signalbox (between 1964 and 1977) remained solely to control the level crossing, and until 14 February 1972 retained two lower quadrant LNWR signals for this purpose, which were replaced on that date by two standard Western Region arms. The level crossing was subsequently converted to unmanned, open automatic status, subject to a 10mph speed restriction. The flashing road signals and audible warning are activated by the train's occupation of the track circuit on the approach side of the crossing. Confirmation that the road traffic signals are working is given to the driver by the flashing white light. There are similar crossings now at Brynmarlais (between Tirydail and Llandebie), Llangadog and Bucknell. Further examples are planned when cash becomes available. Between 1965 and their closure, the former manned crossings at Dolau and Bucknell had the added advantage of being used as unofficial block posts on the 31-mile long single line section between Llandrindod and Craven Arms. Since their closure, trains 'disappear' for up to an hour on this section, the only method of contact between the train and the rest of BR being emergency GPO telephones on each of the unstaffed halts. There is no way in which the passage of the train through the section can be monitored therefore. *Author*

Above: In December 1980 the controversial decision was made to ban the use of main line diesel locomotives between Pantyffynnon and Craven Arms, to allow for delays to track renewals due to financial constraints. The last scheduled locomotive hauled passenger working was a Leeds-Llandrindod Wells weekend excursion on 20 and 21 December 1980. The train was hauled in both directions by Class 40 diesel No 40.030, the only use of this type on an excursion over the route, although No 40.174 assisted an ailing dmu on the 15.38 ex-Shrewsbury as far as Llandrindod on 7 April 1977. No 40.030 is seen heading down the 1 in 90 from Llanbister Road towards the top of the Dolau straight. Note the portable spotlight with the cable leading across the nose of the engine from inside the cab. The return working of this train left Llandrindod on the following afternoon, the stock being stabled in the one remaining siding at Llandrindod, the locomotive having run light to and from Shrewsbury. *Author*

Below: The 14.50 from Shrewsbury arrives at Llanbister Road headed by one of Swansea's reliable Fowler 2-6-4Ts. The village of Llanbister is five miles to the west, via a narrow mountainous lane. The station is of more use, in fact, to the inhabitants of Llangunllo who, although having a station of their own, often prefer the relatively flat if slightly longer journey to Llanbister Road rather than the arduous climb to Llangunllo station. Llanbister Road station marked the beginning of single track (as far as Knighton, with a loop at Llangunllo). The substantial brick building on the former down platform is now used as a private residence. *J. Spencer Gilks*

Right: After a brief 1 in 80 fall to Troedrhiwfedwen Crossing, the line crosses the valley of the River Lugg and climbs up the hillside towards Llangunllo around several sharp reverse curves which, with their 6½in of cant, can be taken at 45mph. This is an extremely attractive section, culminating in a bird's eye view of Llangunllo village in the valley floor whilst the train leans around a half mile long left hand bend. A return WI Day Charter from Llandrindod Wells to Cleethorpes climbs towards Llangunllo behind English Electric Class 37 diesel No 37.181 on 10 May 1977. Before the introduction of the portable headlamps in 1979, spotlight fitted Class 37s were almost exclusively used on trains of this kind (and the local freight to Llandovery). Being based at Pantyffynnon they had to run light between Pantyffynnon and Shrewsbury twice in the day to work such day excursions from the north end of the line. *Author*

Below right: The final curve round the hillside is almost of horseshoe proportions. On 5 June 1964 the down Craven Arms-Llandovery local freight coasts around the curve, headed by Stanier '8F' No 48732. To gain the necessary height, the narrow road from the village to the station takes a circuitous route. Consequently, some of the inhabitants used to take a short cut across the fields. However, this alternative was fraught with danger as a particularly fractious bull had to be negotiated en route, a fact which, no doubt, adversely affected Llangunllo station's receipts! *Derek Cross*

Right: Llangunllo station is a desolate place. Apart from a couple of farmhouses nearby, there is a terrace of railway cottages, the station house and the station itself. It possessed a passing loop until 1965, but no actual signalbox, the necessary levers and instruments being housed in the south end of the station building on the up platform. Stanier '8F' No 48354 pauses on its journey south. Watering facilities were available at Llangunllo, though in winter the pipes were often frozen. In these circumstances it was usual to find a chalked message by the water crane at Knighton, advising trainmen of this fact, so that water could be taken at that point. *John Stratton*

Bottom right: In this view of Llangunllo during the summer of 1964, a Llanelli-Shrewsbury dmu approaches during the first months of dieselisation. Charlie Hammond, one of the signalmen at Llangunllo, was an expert repairer of watches. Consequently, many a broken or revitalised timepiece was put in the guard's custody between Llangunllo and the various locations at the north end of the line. *John Stratton*

Above: The right sort of train with the right engine in the right location. This delightful picture seems to sum up the atmosphere of the 'Central', with a relatively large engine for the load concerned, the engine being one of a handful of regular performers, leaving an isolated station amid superb surroundings. Stanier 'Black 5' No 45406 takes the 11.45 Shrewsbury-Swansea away from Llangunllo on 5 June 1964. In the foreground is the refuge siding used for recessing freight trains. In addition to hauling the last passenger train from Swansea Victoria, this engine's other claim to fame was its use on a Royal Train in 1957, when the Duke of Edinburgh made a long overnight journey from Bangor to Cardigan via the 'Central'. *Derek Cross*

Top right: The summit of the line at 980ft above sea level is 300yd north of Llangunllo station. BR Standard Class 5 No 73023 has brought the 14.40 Shrewsbury-Swansea out of the 647yd curved tunnel and is passing over the peak of the route on 30 April 1964. As a small boy I was told by more than one Shrewsbury driver of the (fictitious) ghost of Llangunllo tunnel who appeared in the early hours of misty mornings above the northern portal of the tunnel to haunt heavy trains coming up the bank from Knighton, causing them violent bouts of slipping near the damp tunnel mouth. The ghost was meant to be the spirit of a former banking engine driver from Knighton who had left the railway in disgrace following an overzealous trip light engine back down the bank from Llangunllo. The purpose of this tale was to try to persuade me to be daft enough to catch the 'up Mail' to Shrewsbury from Llandrindod one suitable night, to return in the early hours of the following day on the 'down Mail' (03.45 ex-Shrewsbury) so that I could witness the existence of this particular spirit first hand! *M. R. C. Price*

Bottom right: The line falls from Llangunllo Summit through the tunnel initially at 1 in 100, steepening to 1 in 60 for four miles. Three quarters of a mile beyond the tunnel exit is Heyope Crossing, where a farm track crosses the railway. There was a water column on the up side just west of the crossing, which was used by northbound freights if no water was available at Llangunllo. BR Standard Class 5 No 73090, with a down passenger train, climbs past the crossing which, now unmanned, is subject to a 10mph speed limit, which represents a considerable inconvenience, being situated on a 1 in 60 incline, especially in view of the negligible use of the farm track which crosses the line simply to gain access to fields. *Sid Morris*

73090

Left: The crossing keeper's cottage at Heyope was not connected to the mains water supply and so water churns were ferried betwen Heyope and Knighton. Knighton's banker crew stop at the crossing to deposit a container for the occupants, who would occasionally find the odd large lump of coal 'accidentally on purpose' dislodged from the tender in their direction. Despite the chain and padlock on the gate, a sex-starved bull (no doubt a relative of the terror of Llangunllo) found his way on to the railway on one occasion, by lifting the gate off its hinges with his horns in an attempt to pursue a herd of cattle in the field opposite the line.
Sid Morris

Below left: The railway runs picturesquely downhill towards Knucklas viaduct, passing the village of Heyope on the opposite side of the valley. During the summer months of 1978 a four-car formation freewheels down the bank seen from Heyope Churchyard. The strengthening of trains causes problems for the guard (if on his own) in working the request halt system (in use since May 1970) as he cannot gain access to the other unit between stations. For this reason, if the train is not too full, he will try to keep one set locked out of use until needed or, some guards (Salop men especially), will try to ensure that local passengers travel in one set (in which he bases himself) and long distance passengers only use the other set. *H. J. Ashman/BR*

Top right: Knucklas viaduct is 190yd long, consists of 13 arches, is up to 75ft above ground level, and is one of the most architecturally attractive viaducts in the country. Not that the fireman of this Saltney-Pontardulais freight train will have had much opportunity to view its scenic splendour as he and the unassisted Stanier '8F' toil up the climb towards Llangunllo. *Derek Cross*

Bottom right: The same train, a few yards earlier, which gives you some impression of its speed (or lack of it!). The viaduct's major features of interest are the castellated towers at each end, and the embellished parapets. The viaduct is overlooked to the north-west by the hilltop mound of Knucklas Castle, and it is said that some of the stone used in the viaduct was carried from the remains of the castle. *Derek Cross*

48739

Left: An unusual ground level view of a train coasting across the viaduct, in this case Fowler 2-6-4T No 42390, with the 10.25 Swansea-Shrewsbury (always a well-patronised train), the date being 19 August 1959. Not having to brake for a station stop at Knucklas, the train was probably doing at least the 45mph limit for the section between Llanbister Road and Knighton. The load of six coaches was the theoretical maximum for a Class 4 locomotive over the line unassisted. Another legend related to the viaduct tells of a fox which was being chased across the bridge by a pack of hounds and took the decision to jump over the parapet, falling to its death 75ft below rather than being savaged to death by its pursuers. Whether the fox was acting in a self destructory fashion or just made a drastic mistake is a matter for conjecture. *J. Spencer Gilks*

Below left: A Stanier '8F' negotiates the curve between Knucklas viaduct and the station on 5 June 1964, with a Swansea Eastern Depot-Salop Coton Hill goods. This curve once formed a part of a 'Prize Length' — the permanent way department's equivalent of the 'Best Kept Station' award. The track along the line is still maintained by hand, basically. The vast majority of the mileage between Pantyffynnon and Craven Arms is composed of bullhead rails on wooden sleepers. The various gangs have to be versatile in hedge cutting, fence building, sleeper changing, lifting and packing, painting and various other duties needing ingenuity. They are lucky to have inherited such a well-designed infrastructure from the original contractors, who used considerable initiative also; for example; fossilised trees were laid beneath the ballast to cross marshy ground and some of the overbridges have a layer of 'shock absorbing' clay between the ballast and the masonry. *Derek Cross*

Above: In late 1959 two Fairburn 2-6-4T engines Nos 42296 and 42645 were transferred to Landore shed Swansea followed, in 1960, by No 42182. The reason for this move was that Landore was experiencing problems keeping the 'foreign' and ageing Fowler 2-6-4Ts in working order (following their re-allocation as a result of the closure of Paxton Street depot). On 14 April 1961, No 42182 restarts from Knucklas on the 1 in 60 bank, with the 14.50 Shrewsbury-Swansea. The locomotive provided for this train would have worked the 06.15 Swansea-Shrewsbury the same morning. Before the closure of Paxton Street shed the trainmen used to work the 10.25 Swansea through to Shrewsbury and return with the 14.40 from Shrewsbury, having relief opposite Paxton Street shed (to save overtime). *IAL*

Below: With only a couple of weeks left of regular steam passenger working on the line, Stanier 'Black 5' No 45190 passes through the deserted platform at Knucklas. The patronage of the station has increased considerably following the construction of a council housing estate between the railway and the village, as well as the new service from May 1970 which theoretically improved the position of many of the smaller halts by making them request stops on most, if not all, of the trains concerned. Previous to this only a couple of nominated trains would call at some of these less used halts. The station building at Knucklas developed a disconcerting list towards the track in its final years. *Derek Cross*

Left: The same train seen heading down the valley towards Knighton. Offa's Dyke runs along the top of the hill in the background, whilst in front of the engine can be seen the trackbed of the three sidings that constituted Knucklas Goods Yard, which could accommodate a total of 45 wagons. It is hard to imagine four wagons being in the yard, let alone 45! *Derek Cross*

Centre left: The basic pattern of passenger services over the route for several decades consisted of Swansea-Shrewsbury trains, Swansea-Pontardulais and Llanelli-Llandovery 'locals', and some Llandovery-Builth Road-Knighton-Craven Arms local trains. Here is seen the 14.20 Craven Arms-Llandovery climbing towards Knucklas, powered by one of Paxton Street's Fowler 2-6-4Ts on 26 June 1950. The van behind the engine was so marshalled that it could be detached easily from the rear of the return working (the 18.05 Llandovery-Craven Arms) and re-attached to the rear of the 19.50 Hereford-Shrewsbury. *G. A. Hookham*

Bottom left: On 4 August 1914 relatives on both platforms at Knighton prepare to send off local Territorials to war. The down train is pulling out of the refuge loop, whilst the up train includes through coaches to London Euston (via Stafford). Knighton has always been a relatively busy station, especially on Thursdays (Market Day). The station is on the English side of the River Teme, though the town is in Wales. The double track from south of the station stretched to Craven Arms. There were two signalboxes: number 2 box can be seen here on the down platform, whilst number 1 box was around the corner, towards Bucknell, controlling the entrance to the down refuge loop and goods yard. The large stone building with its patterned roof is now used exclusively as a private residence and office. *M. Cadwallader collection*

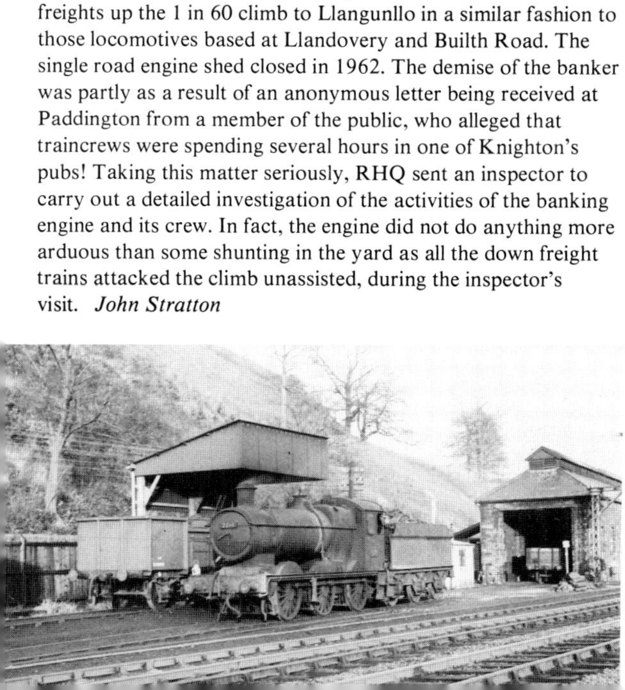

Below: The Knighton banker was provided to assist southbound freights up the 1 in 60 climb to Llangunllo in a similar fashion to those locomotives based at Llandovery and Builth Road. The single road engine shed closed in 1962. The demise of the banker was partly as a result of an anonymous letter being received at Paddington from a member of the public, who alleged that traincrews were spending several hours in one of Knighton's pubs! Taking this matter seriously, RHQ sent an inspector to carry out a detailed investigation of the activities of the banking engine and its crew. In fact, the engine did not do anything more arduous than some shunting in the yard as all the down freight trains attacked the climb unassisted, during the inspector's visit. *John Stratton*

Above: On 5 June 1964 Stanier 'Black 5' No 45190 takes water at Knighton prior to the dash towards Craven Arms with the 10.25 Swansea-Shrewsbury. To fill up with water at Knighton on a tender engine was 'conditional', depending on whether water had been taken at Llandovery or Builth Road. For tank engines, however, the filling of tanks was 'mandatory' at Knighton, and I well remember one amusing incident in the early 1960s, shortly before the demise of 'old faithful' Fowler tank No 42305. Having been transferred to Landore shed, the locomotive was not in the best of health but, being a Swansea engine, it was allocated to its booked job of the 14.50 passenger from Shrewsbury. We crept to Knighton where, despite the situation, comic relief was provided by the driver who managed to entice an immaculately dressed travelling ticket inspector in to a position near the water crane at the end of the down platform. The fireman, with admirable timing, allowed the tanks to overflow and flung the gushing pipe back towards the platform. The result, of course, was one extremely damp ticket inspector. In fact, as a result of the engine's condition, the train was piloted from Knighton by the banking engine, despite the load of only four coaches. *Derek Cross*

Left: 'That it should come to this!' With the ban on large locos, engineering trains, when required, have to be trimmed to suit the capabilities of Class 03 shunting engines. On 5 July 1981, No 03.145 and 03.151 (worked in multiple) ran, at a maximum speed of 28mph, from Llanelli to Craven Arms and back, dropping most of the contents of their two 'sealions' of ballast north of Knighton. I would think that 220 miles in a day is a record for this type of loco. Indeed, whilst seen here at Knighton, the driver put several gallons of water in the radiator of the rear loco. Locally nicknamed 'Ivor the Engine and his mate Charlie', they presented quite a comical view 'at speed' with their whirring side rods. Of course, all the level crossings and signalboxes on the line were specially opened for this Sunday working, although most of the work was confined to the immediate south of Craven Arms. Ironically, more ballast could have been unloaded more economically by using a main line engine, saving the cost of several repeat performances on subsequent Sundays of this '03' operation to complete the task. *Author*

Knighton-Shrewsbury

Left: The 10.25 Swansea-Shrewsbury passes Bucknell up distant signal on 5 June 1964, hauled by one of Shrewsbury's Stanier 'Jubilee' (6P/5F) class locomotives which were a relatively common sight during the final months of steam on the line's passenger services. The layout of the route between Knighton and Craven Arms gives rise to fast running and this particular train was only allowed 17 minutes to cover the $12\frac{3}{4}$ miles (including a station stop at Bucknell). This section was singled in 1965, an important date for the line since most of the intermediate stations were unmanned and passing loops closed in that year. The Electric Token Block system was replaced by the less flexible, but far cheaper, Staff and Ticket system for controlling the single line sections. *Derek Cross*

Above: From a point between Knucklas and Knighton (at the bottom of the 1 in 60 gradient) to Bucknell, the railway keeps close company with the River Teme. The then thrice weekly Craven Arms-Llandovery local goods trundles along the valley between Bucknell and Knighton with Stanier '8F' No 48362 providing the power, tender first, on 12 June 1964. In earlier years there were two 'locals' (as this train was called); one ran from Craven Arms to Llandovery, crossing the reverse working en route, latterly at Llandrindod Wells. The reason for the down train being hauled tender first was that the turntable at Craven Arms was too short to cope with a Stanier '8F'. The locomotive off the 'down local' would work on banking duties from Llandovery during the night.
Derek Cross

Right: The 'down local' seen after leaving Bucknell on 5 June 1964, behind Stanier '8F' No 48732. When the 'down local' used to run on Saturdays, a strange ailment would often suddenly strike the engine as it approached Llandrindod on its way home. On arriving at Llandrindod, the Llandovery driver would tell the shunter that the engine was a failure and that he would have to put the train off in the refuge loop and proceed to Llandovery light engine. This, of course, was all planned to give the crew an early finish.
Derek Cross

Right: The staff at Bucknell line up for an official photograph as a down passenger train runs in to the station. The station building is the most architecturally pleasing on the route, with its fine stone work and steep gables. Thankfully it remains today almost exactly as shown here, being used now as a private dwelling. The signalbox on the end of the up platform was subsequently replaced by a more modern design. *Lens of Sutton*

Below: The Stanier '8Fs' were the last steam locomotives to work over the route as they continued to appear on the local freight from Pantyffynnon to Craven Arms (which effectively replaced the Llandovery-Craven Arms workings). This train was steam hauled after the end of passenger steam in 1964. Stanier '8F' No 48307, with its 87F shedplate, passes through Bucknell heading north. Following the closure of first Paxton Street shed and then the East Dock depot, this class was based at Llanelli, until transferred away from South Wales. Some, in the company of certain of the BR Standard 2-6-4Ts found new work on the Somerset & Dorset line. The last official steam working over the route was the 08.45 Pantyffynnon-Craven Arms 'local' hauled by '8F' No 48732 on 21 May 1965. *Derek Cross*

Left: After its closure as a block post, up until the conversion of the level crossing to automatic open status, the box controlled the passage of trains across the roadway (albeit without the use of fixed signals — hence the provision of stop boards). On three occasions during this time, however, dmus ran into the gates, causing varying amounts of damage. The first occasion involved an experimental run with one of the 1963 vintage Swindon Inter City units which, comprising two power cars only, allegedly covered the 25 miles from Llandrindod in 30 minutes and collided with the gates before the crossing keeper had a chance to open same. The second occasion was as a result of the late arrival of the crossing keeper due to transport difficulties in thick fog. The story goes that the driver of the 'down Mail' (03.44 ex-Shrewsbury) tried to encourage the gates to open with not so gentle assistance from the buffers of his dmu! The final occurrence was when the 09.59 Swansea-Shrewsbury over-ran the platform on 7 April 1977. The gates were never fully repaired after this final 'contretemps' as the crossing was automated some months later. The 15.38 Shrewsbury-Swansea approaches with caution from the north, watched by Signalmen Bird and Powell.
Sid Morris

Left: The yard at Bucknell outlived that at neighbouring Knighton by several months. After the withdrawal of the 'local' goods north of Llandrindod Wells, Bucknell continued to be served by a local trip from Hereford which ran round at Craven Arms and was usually hauled by 'Hymek' class diesel. A conference appears to be taking place in this picture regarding the contents of the vanfit attached to Stanier '8F' No 48409. The date is 5 June 1964.
Derek Cross

Top left: Hopton Heath, viewed from the road bridge which spans the north end of the station. The signalbox on the up platform was replaced in 1945 by a structure on the bank between the down line and goods yard. In the background the line can be seen curving on to a long straight which leads towards Bucknell past Bedstone School and over Adley Crossing. This section is renowned for the number of pheasants seen scratching around the track, the more unfortunate of whom have occasionally been known to end up on the dinner table of a certain member of the Salop traincrew establishment.
Mowat Collection

Top right: In later years the signalbox at Hopton Heath was only opened on an 'as required' basis for gaining access to the goods yard. Three signals in the 'off' position on the same post north of the station indicate that the box is 'switched out'. This sharing of the one post was to aid visibility, the arm for the up 'starter' being situated on the wrong side of the line in order to be seen from beyond the stone bridge. *John Stratton*

Above: Because of the position of the lead from the down line into the yard the down platform is staggered to the north of the up platform and extends underneath the overbridge. Owing to the limited platform width under the bridge, there used to be an instruction for guards to prevent passengers from detraining on to this narrow part of the platform. On St Valentine's Day in 1981 the 12.25 Swansea-Shrewsbury calls to set down a couple of shoppers who had made their weekly trip to Knighton. *Author*

Left: Stanier '8F' No 48732, with the 12.30 Swansea-Shrewsbury, approaches Broome on 8 July 1953. The gated goods yard on the up side was located at a substantially lower level than the main line which, having crossed the River Clun, climbs at 1 in 80 through the station. Between Hopton Heath and Broome the railway passes west of the village at Clungunford. It is rather surprising that the Knighton Railway Co did not build the line nearer this settlement, which is the largest between Bucknell and Craven Arms. *G. A. Hookham*

Below: The down platform at Broome was of wooden construction and, in later years, was not too sound, as is shown by the barrier being passed by No 73097, one of the line's most commonly seen BR Standard Class 5 engines. When the line between Knighton and Craven Arms was singled in 1965 the down line was retained to become the single track until just south of Broome, where the formation was slewed on to the former up line to avoid using the inferior platform at Broome. The train shown is the 12.00 Shrewsbury-Swansea on 2 September 1963. *Andrew Muckley*

Far left: The Central Wales line joins the 'North and West' Newport-Hereford-Shrewsbury route at Craven Arms, after negotiating a right angled bend. This summer Saturday down train has just left the down 'North and West' line and is climbing around the curve towards Broome. The present junction is situated nearer the station; the remaining single line leads towards the now disused down bay platform before trailing into the up 'North and West' line through a pair of spring points at the south end of the up platform. The junction box at Craven Arms closed in 1965 and, since this time, down Central Wales trains, after obtaining the single line staff (or ticket) at Craven Arms Crossing box (north of the station), cross over on to the up line. Once station duties have been completed the guard operates a ground frame (released by the crossing box) to reverse and lock the spring points leading to 'the Central', before lowering the starting signal. Once the train has cleared the main line the guard restores the levers to the normal position, locks the ground frame, checks with the signalman by telephone, and then walks down the line to rejoin his train before giving the 'right away' to the driver. *Sid Morris*

Above left: For many years the 10.25 from Swansea and 14.40 from Shrewsbury conveyed a tea car south of Craven Arms. In this August 1939 scene, Stanier 'Black 5' No 5383 backs down on to the 14.40 after picking up the tea car. Prior to Nationalisation this train also conveyed through coaches from Euston to Swansea, having worked from London to Stafford attached to the down 'Manxman' express. The tea car was not dissimilar in concept to BRs new Micro Buffet, the former having two compartments converted in to use as a serving area. *G. A. Hookham*

Left: The final 20 miles along the 'main line' is characterised by the climb to, and descent from, Church Stretton. Nearing the top of the bank is BR Standard Class 5 No 73025 with the 10.25 Swansea-Shrewsbury on 25 April 1964. Central Wales trains never called at the smaller intermediate stations north of Craven Arms, other than Church Stretton. *Derek Cross*

Above: Stanier '8F' No 48474 starts the descent towards Craven Arms from near Little Stretton, with a down empty mineral wagon train. The horizon on the left is formed by Long Mynd, which rises above the west side of the Church Stretton gorge through which the railway passes. For up trains the 12 miles from Church Stretton to Shrewsbury is a final dash, to accomplish as early an arrival time as possible. *Derek Cross*

Right: The 2V64 headcode denotes a down train for 'the Central' — in fact, the 12.25 Shrewsbury-Llanelli on Saturday, 4 July 1964, hauled by BR Standard 2-6-4T No 80069. The location is Sutton Bridge Junction south of Shrewsbury. *A. W. Martin*

Many photographs have been taken, and much has been written, about Shrewsbury as a railway centre. To Central Wales passengers it has always represented a kind of 'Iron Curtain' or 'gateway to the unknown'. The 'local' feels a sense of anxiety on leaving the relative security of a terminating Central Wales train for the change to a 'main line' train destined for urban areas. Conversely, no doubt, some of the occupants of the three coaches seen here in platform 2 are feeling safe in the knowledge that they are heading home on the 14.40 to Swansea. The locomotive on the stopblock, and the three carriages, would have worked the 10.25 from Swansea. Prior to the rundown during the early and mid-1960s, Central Wales trains would detach or attach through coaches for and from such places as Liverpool, Manchester, Leeds and Stafford. This pattern of working became confined chiefly to summer Saturdays, with the notable exception of the Swansea-York Mail, which continued on a six day basis up to June 1964, from which date this train's Welsh starting point became Aberystwyth. *Derek Cross*

Left: Shrewsbury station's appearance was transformed by the removal of the overall roof and, whilst this unquestionably led to a brighter and more pleasant atmosphere, the character of the station was ruined in some sense. This more recent photograph is unusual in that it depicts a locomotive hauled Central Wales train (in platform 6), deputising for a dmu. The reason for this was the heatwave in 1976, which caused the partial replacement of the 'gasping' dmus by locomotives and coaches for a few weeks. Watering cans, fire buckets and at least one garden hose were marshalled to meet all dmus at the few remaining staffed stations, in order to replenish boiling radiators. No 37.182 is the substituting diesel concerned here, on 29 June 1976, with the 15.41 to Swansea. *Author*

The Branches

The Llanmorlais Branch

Above and below: Two views of Penclawdd station, looking towards the Llanmorlais terminus. The branch was single tracked for its five miles. The local freight train from Gowerton is seen here, hauled by GWR's '57xx' pannier tank on 2 August 1957, one month before the closure of the line. Opened in 1867 to Penclawdd, and extended to Llanmorlais by 1877, its passenger service was withdrawn in 1931. *Both: Hugh Davies*

Above: Llanmorlais station in 1957. The line continued around the curve to reach a colliery. Several sidings were served along the branch, notably Baldwin's Elba Steelworks just west of Gowerton, and a Royal Ordnance Factory west of Penclawdd. *Hugh Davies*

The Llanelli Line

Below: Llanelli shed plays host on 23 July 1961 to a forlorn looking Fowler 2-6-4T No 42305. This particular loco spent its entire working life on the line following its construction in 1927, along with other members of this class. It was an arduous life for a tank engine, employed on duties more commonly performed by tender engines. *J. C. Haydon*

Right: Bynea and Llangennech are the only stations between Llanelli and Pontardulais. In this view of the former, looking north, can be seen, in the background, the connection leading to a scrapyard on the banks of the Loughor, where various steam locomotives met their end. *Lens of Sutton*

Below: The 10.10 Swansea to Shrewsbury five-car dmu pauses at the desolate station at Llangennech, which is situated adjacent to marshland between the Loughor Estuary and the village. *Author*

Left: On the western bank of the Loughor Estuary the 10.10 Swansea to Shrewsbury heads towards Morlais Junction. The Swansea District line to Court Sart Junction climbs to the right in order to cross the Estuary, whilst the single (former up) Pontardulais line heads straight on past Morlais Colliery towards Hendy Junction. There used to be a flying junction arrangement at Morlais whereby down Pontardulais trains curved sharply underneath the District line to feed in to the latter's down track at Morlais Junction itself. Routed towards Pontardulais, off the main line, Central Wales trains receive 'the feathers' junction indication on the controlling signal. *Author*

Below: No 6818 *Hardwick Grange* leaves the close confines of Hendy tunnel on 24 March 1962 with an excursion from the then officially closed Brynamman West to Cardiff in connection with the Wales-France Rugby International. The train will shortly turn left at Hendy Junction and climb the third side of the triangle on to the Swansea District or 'New Line' as it is often called. *H. Daniel*

The Brynamman Branch

Above and below: Two views of Brynamman West, terminus of the branch from Pantyffynnon. The first shows a Stephenson Locomotive Society Push/Pull Special in July 1955, powered by LMS 'Jinty' 0-6-0 No 47480 (out of sight). A few yards beyond the road bridge in the background was the ex-Midland Railway station of Brynamman East, served by trains to and from Swansea St Thomas. Though there was a line between the two stations, it was never utilised by passenger trains. The second photograph shows stock off a local train from Pantyffynnon reversing out of the station in May 1958. The passenger service was curtailed three months later, and the section from Garnant closed completely in December 1963.
Real Photographs/Hugh Davies

Gwaun-cae-Gurwen Branch

Right, top and bottom: Two views of GCG (as it is known). There was a passenger service between Garnant and Gwaun-cae-Gurwen from 1908 to 1926. In fact, the trains (formed by a GWR steam railcar) were suspended during the General Strike and never restored. The halt was just south of the level crossing and footbridge seen beyond the 'Jinty' and its enthusiasts' Special train. The sidings layout seen in the background, beyond the footbridge, towards the open cast loading site, remains basically the same today, the branch still being used by coal trains. The alignment now used dates from 1907, when the original route from Garnant to Gwaun-cae-Gurwen was superseded. *Real Photographs/Hugh Davies*

47480

The Abernant Branch

Above: The line to Abernant Colliery leaves the Gwaun-cae-Gurwen branch approximately $\frac{1}{4}$ mile before the level crossing at Gwaun-cae-Gurwen. In 1911 the GWR had authorised a plan to continue the branch southwards to Felin Fran on the Swansea District Line. A couple of stations were even constructed on the proposed through route, although these were never opened as the plan did not materialise. Diesels Nos 37.177 and 37.208 grind to a halt at the stopboard near the junction with the Gwaun-cae-Gurwen line. In the background can be seen one of the abortive stations (complete with awning) which was to have served Gwaun-cae-Gurwen. *R. E. Ruffell*

Top right: Abernant Colliery was opened in 1960 and is a considerable source of traffic for British Rail. Much of the coal from this anthracite belt having been tripped to Pantyffynnon, is then forwarded to Swansea Docks. *BR*

The Carmarthen Line

Bottom right: The line from Llandilo to Carmarthen was $14\frac{1}{4}$ miles in length and joined the line from Aberystwyth at Abergwili Junction from where the LNWR had running powers to reach Carmarthen Town station. Nantgaredig was one of the three intermediate stations which had a passing loop (shown here looking west in July 1956). *H. C. Casserley*

NANTCAREDIC

Top: Llanarthney was unstaffed in 1954, the loop having been removed before World War 2. In latter years the trains were worked by GWR pannier tanks of the '74xx' variety, an example of which is seen here with its solitary coach on 3 September 1963, the line's final year. *Andrew Muckley*

Above: Drysllwyn station on 13 July 1956. This line was opened in 1864 by the Llanelly Dock & Railway Company, and was operated by the LNWR from 1871. The pastoral nature of the landscape through which it passed gives a clue to one of the major traffics, as does an 1898 Weekly Operating Notice showing a 14.00 and 15.30 Cattle Train from Carmarthen to Shrewsbury, as a consequence of Carmarthen Fair. *H. C. Casserley*

Above: Scenically not dissimilar from the 'main line' section between Llandilo and Llandovery, the Carmarthen line paralleled the meandering River Towy. In July 1962 GWR pannier tank No 7439 heads upstream with Dryslwyn Castle in the background. *IAL*

Left: Golden Grove, viewed from the rear of a down train for Carmarthen. Business was boosted here when the Royal Welsh Agricultural Show was held in nearby fields. The LNWR lower quadrant signal was still in situ in 1980! *H. C. Casserley*

Bottom left: The final intermediate station before Llandilo was Llandilo Bridge. In the background can be seen the profile of the Central Wales line. The Carmarthen line joined the main line just south of the river bridge across the Towy. It was a useful short cut to and from West Wales and, up to its closure, was used by certain summer Saturday trains between Shrewsbury, Tenby and Pembroke Dock.
H. C. Casserley

Selected track plans (based on LMS sketches, circa 1925)

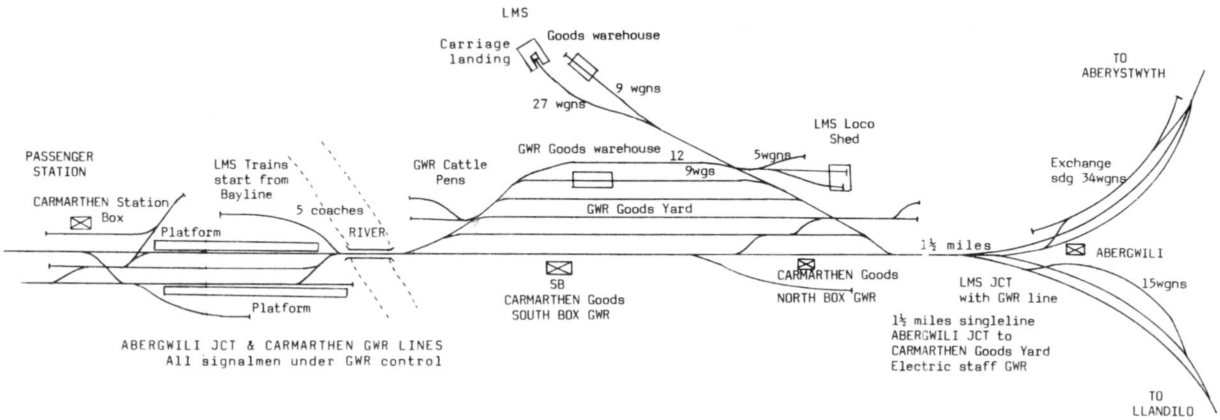

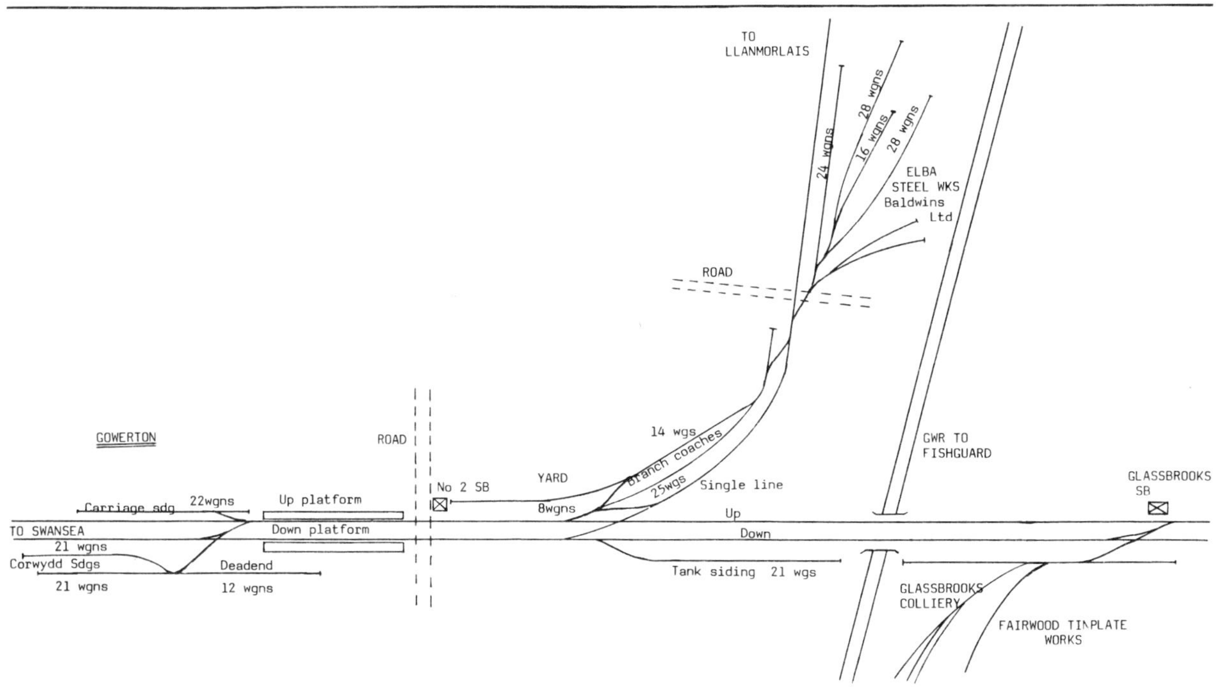

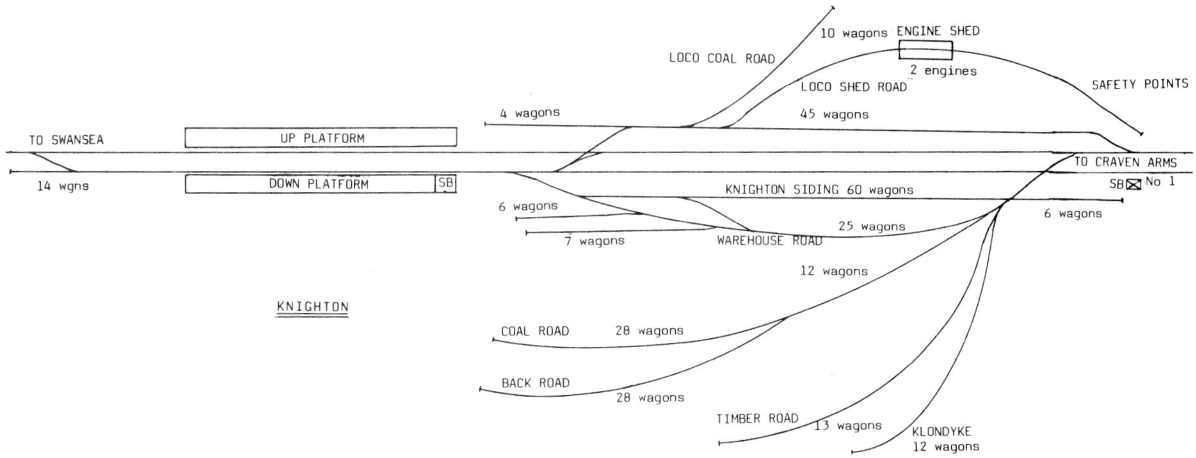
KNIGHTON
TO SWANSEA
14 wgns
UP PLATFORM
DOWN PLATFORM
SB
4 wagons
LOCO COAL ROAD
10 wagons
ENGINE SHED
2 engines
LOCO SHED ROAD
45 wagons
SAFETY POINTS
TO CRAVEN ARMS
SB No 1
KNIGHTON SIDING 60 wagons
6 wagons
6 wagons
7 wagons
WAREHOUSE ROAD
25 wagons
12 wagons
COAL ROAD
28 wagons
BACK ROAD
28 wagons
TIMBER ROAD
13 wagons
KLONDYKE
12 wagons

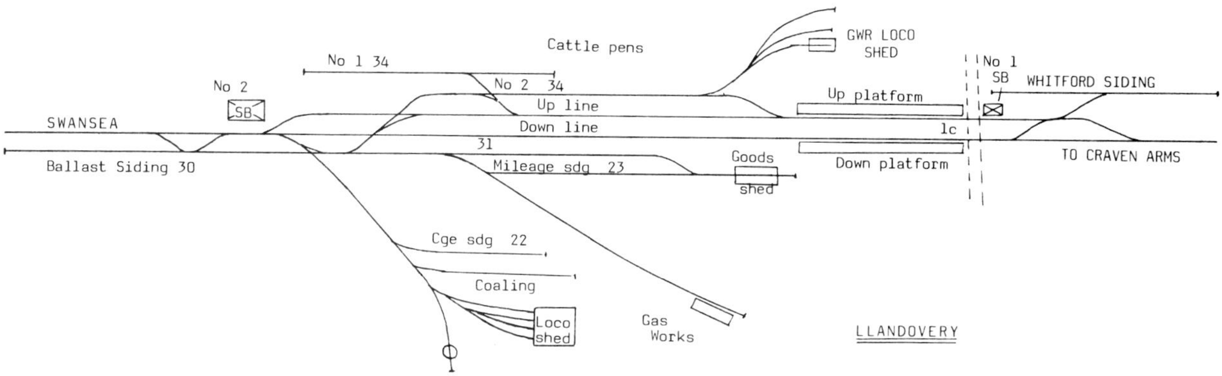
No 1 34
Cattle pens
GWR LOCO SHED
No 2
SB
No 2 34
Up line
Up platform
No 1
SB
WHITFORD SIDING
SWANSEA
Down line
1c
31
Ballast Siding 30
Mileage sdg 23
Goods shed
Down platform
TO CRAVEN ARMS
Cge sdg 22
Coaling
Loco shed
Gas Works
LLANDOVERY

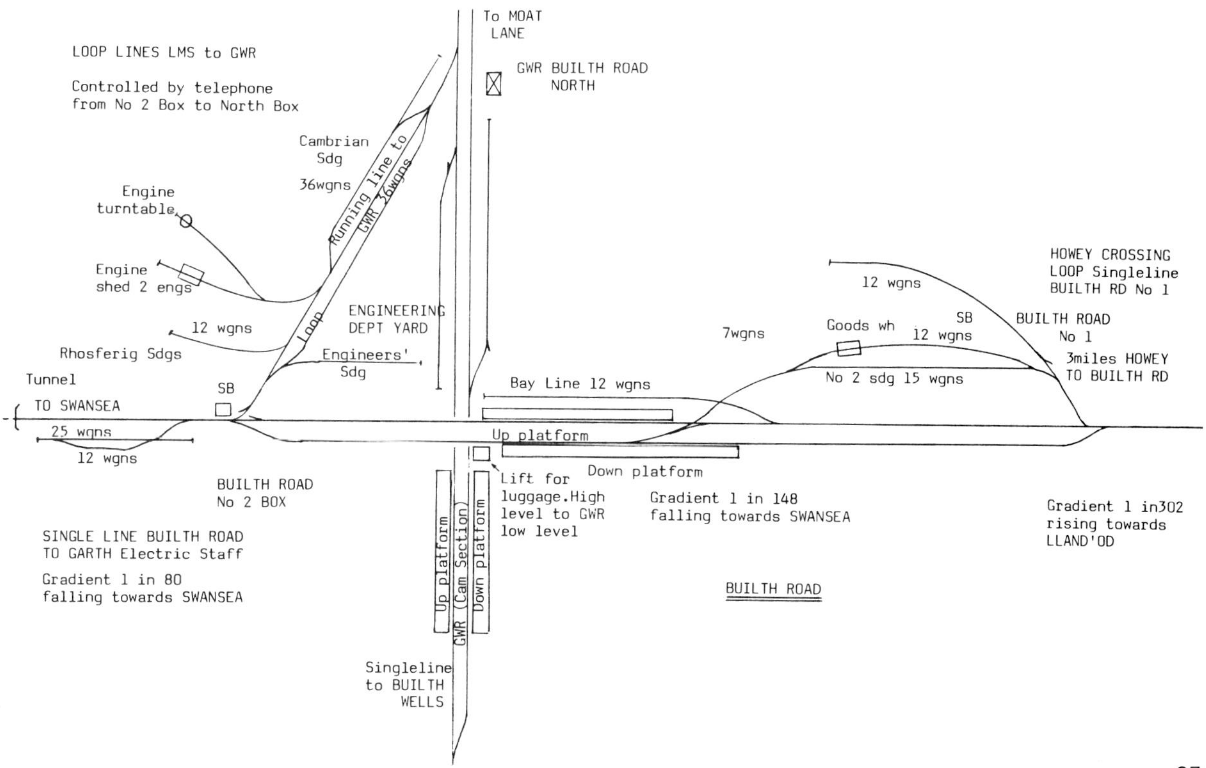
To MOAT LANE
LOOP LINES LMS to GWR
Controlled by telephone from No 2 Box to North Box
GWR BUILTH ROAD NORTH
Cambrian Sdg
36wgns
Running line to GWR 36wgns
Engine turntable
Engine shed 2 engs
12 wgns
Rhosferig Sdgs
Loop
ENGINEERING DEPT YARD
Engineers' Sdg
Tunnel
TO SWANSEA
SB
25 wgns
12 wgns
HOWEY CROSSING LOOP Singleline BUILTH RD No 1
12 wgns
SB
BUILTH ROAD No 1
7wgns
Goods wh
12 wgns
3miles HOWEY TO BUILTH RD
No 2 sdg 15 wgns
Bay Line 12 wgns
Up platform
Down platform
Lift for luggage.High level to GWR low level
BUILTH ROAD No 2 BOX
SINGLE LINE BUILTH ROAD TO GARTH Electric Staff
Gradient 1 in 80 falling towards SWANSEA
Up platform
GWR (Cam Section)
Down platform
Gradient 1 in 148 falling towards SWANSEA
Gradient 1 in302 rising towards LLAND'OD
Singleline to BUILTH WELLS
BUILTH ROAD

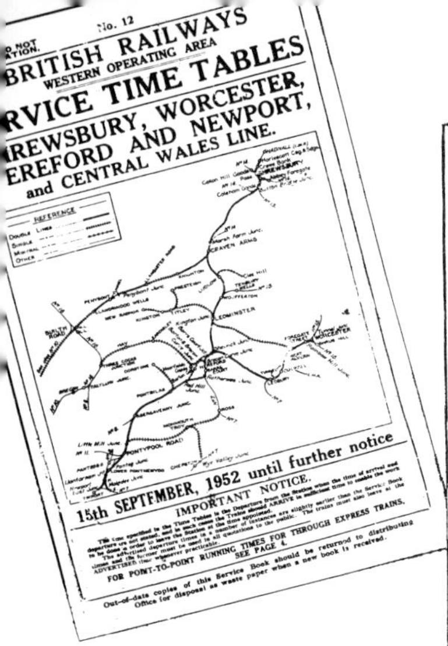

Extracts from Working Timetable — Winter 1952/3

LIST OF SIGNAL BOXES—continued.

Distance Box to Box.		NAME OF BOX.	TIMES DURING WHICH BOXES ARE OPEN. Week Days. Opened. Mondays.	Week Days. Opened. Other Days.	Week Days. Closed at	Sundays. Opened at	Sundays. Closed at	Whether Provided with Switch.
		CRAVEN ARMS (Central Wales Junction exclusive) AND SWANSEA (Victoria).						
—	—	Broome	7.30 a.m.	7.30 a.m.	2.40 p.m.	—	—	Yes.
2	45½	Hopton Heath	As required.	As required.		—	—	Yes.
2	66¼	Bucknell	1 50 a.m.	—	—	—	After last train Sunday morning.	No.
4	1	Knighton No. 1	As required.	As required.		—	—	Yes.
—	21	Knighton No. 2	2. 5 a.m.	—	—	—	After last	No.
6	36	Llangunllo	2.45 a.m.	—	—	—	train Sunday	No.
2	73	Llanbister Road	3.20 a.m.	—	—	—	morning.	No.
3	52½	Dolau Station	9.10 a.m.	9.10 a.m.	4.20 p.m.	—	—	Yes.
2	33¾	Penybont Junction	3.25 a.m.	—	—	—	After last	No.
—	46¼	Penybont	3.25 a.m.	—	—	—	train Sunday	No.
3	12¼	Llandrindod No. 1	3.35 a.m.	—	—	—	morning.	No.
—	37	Llandrindod No. 2	3.35 a.m.	—	—	—		No.
2	61¼	Howey	3.45 a.m.	—	—	—		No.
2	57	Builth Road No. 1	3.50 a.m.	—	—	—		No.
—	28	Builth Road No. 2	3.50 a.m.	—	—	—	After last	No.
5	14¾	Garth	4.20 a.m.	—	—	—	train Sunday	No.
5	2¼	Llanwrtyd Wells	4.35 a.m.	—	—	—	morning.	No.
2	70½	Sugar Loaf Summit	4.50 a.m.	—	—	—		No.
3	63¾	Cynghordy	5. 5 a.m.	—	—	—		No.
4	55½	Llandovery North	5.15 a.m.	—	—	—		No.
—	28	Llandovery South	5.15 a.m.	—	—	—		No.
3	33½	Llanwrda	5.45 a.m.	—	—	—		No.
1	62	Llangadock	5.55 a.m.	—	—	—	After	No.
5	42¼	Llandilo North	6. 0 a.m.	—	—	—	last train.	No.
—	15½	Llandilo South	6.10 a.m.	—	—	—		No.
—	40¾	Carmarthen Valley Junction ..	6.10 a.m.	—	—	—		No.
—	28	Ffairfach	6. 0 a.m.	—	—	—	After last train.	No.
2	52	Derwydd Road	6. 0 a.m.	5.30 a.m.	7.55 p.m.	8.30 a.m. —	C —	Yes.
—	47¾	Cilyrychen Crossing	5.55 a.m.	—	—	—	After last Freight train Sunday morning.	No.
—	67¾	Llandebie	5.55 a.m.	—	—	8.25 a.m. 2.30 p.m. —	B C After last Freight train Sunday morning.	No.
1	64½	Tirydail	5.50 a.m.	—	—	8.25 a.m. 2.30 p.m. —	B C After last Freight train Sunday morning.	No.
—	66	Pantyffynnon North	5.50 a.m.	—	—	8.20 a.m. 2.35 p.m. —	B C After last Freight train Sunday morning.	No.
—	37	Pantyffynnon South	5.40 a.m.	—	—	8.20 a.m. 2.35 p.m. —	B C After last Freight train Sunday morning.	Yes.
3	60½	Glynhir Siding	As required.	As required.		8.10 a.m. 2.40 p.m. —	B C —	Yes.
—	41½	Pontardulais Junction North ..	5.45 a.m.	—	—	—	4. 0 a.m. **N**	Yes.
—	32¾	Pontardulais Junction Station	5.30 a.m.	—	—	—	After last Freight train Sunday morning.	No.
—	§43	Pontardulais	6. 0 a.m.	—	—	8. 5 a.m. 2.45 p.m. —	B C After last train Sunday morning.	No.
—	49¼	Birch Rock Siding	As required.	As required.	—	—	—	Yes.
1	10¼	Grovesend Colliery Sidings ..	As required.	As required.	—	—	—	Yes.
1	24¼	Gorseinon No. 1	7. 0 a.m.	7. 0 a.m	11. 0 p.m. **SX** 7Z0 p.m. **SO**	—	—	Yes.
—	32½	Gorseinon No. 2	6. 0 a.m.	—	—	—	After last train Sunday morning.	No.
1	14¼	Glasbrooks Sidings	As required	As required.	—	—	—	Yes.
—	19½	Gowerton South No. 2 ..	6. 0 a.m.	—	—	—	After last train Sunday morning.	No.
1	43¼	Dunvant	6.30 a.m.	6.30 a.m.	¶	—	—	Yes.
3	15¾	Mumbles Road	6. 0 a.m.	6. 0 a.m.	5.30 p.m.	—	—	Yes.
1	34¾	Swansea Bay 1	10.50 a.m.	10.50 a.m.	12.50 p.m.	—	—	Yes.
—	17½	Swansea Bay 2	6. 0 a.m.	—	—	—	After last	No.
—	31	„ 1	5.45 a.m.	—	—	—	train Sunday	Yes.
—	22½	„ 2	6. 0 a.m.	—	—	—	morning.	Yes.
—	16	„ 3	6. 0 a.m.	6. 0 a.m.	10.20 p.m. or last Train.	—	—	No.

A—Or after 10.25 p.m. Worcester Freight has cleared. **B**—Closed after clearing of 8.5 a.m. Empty Milk Tanks, Llanelly to Ffairfach. **C**—Closed after clearing of 5.30 p.m. Milk, Ffairfach to Llanelly. **N—Or after last train performing work has left.** **Z**—Or after 6.30 p.m. Passenger Swansea (Vic.) to York has cleared. **§—Distance from Pontardulais Level Crossing 11 chains.** ¶—After clearance of last Down Passenger Train.

MAXIMUM SPEED OF TRAINS THROUGH JUNCTIONS AND AT OTHER SPECIFIED PLACES

Name of Place.	From	To	Miles per hour
CRAVEN ARMS AND SWANSEA (Victoria)			
	UP TRAINS.		
Between Swansea (Vic). and Gowerton South	All Trains		35
Through Gowerton Junction	All Trains		20
Gowerton South and Pontardulais	All Trains		45
Pontardulais Junction	Swansea (Victoria)	Llandovery	15
Pontardulais and Pantyffynnon	Between 8m. 75ch. and 9m. 5ch.		50
Pantyffynnon	Double Line	Brynamman Branch	10
Derwydd Road	Through Station		15
Derwydd Road and Ffairfach	Between 15¼m.p. and 16m. 30c.		30
,, ,, ,, ,,	Between 16m. 30c. and 17¼ m.p.		20
Carmarthen Valley Junction	Carmarthen	Llandilo	10
Glanrhyd Halt and Llangadock	For heavy engines only		20
Between Sugar Loaf and Builth Road.	All Trains		50
Between Builth Road and Llandrindod Wells.	All Trains		45
Between Llandrindod Wells and Llanbister Road.	All Trains		55
Between Llanbister Road and Llangunllo.	All Trains		45
Llangunllo Tunnel to Knighton	Passenger Trains		45
	Freight Trains		20
Knighton, through Station	All Trains		30
Between Knighton and Craven Arms.	All Trains		55
South end of Craven Arms Station over Curve.	All Trains		10
CRAVEN ARMS AND SWANSEA (Victoria).—DOWN TRAINS.			
South end of Craven Arms Station over Curve.	All Trains		10
Craven Arms and Knighton	All Trains		55
At Knighton—through Station	All Trains		30
Llangunllo and Llanbister Road	All Trains		45
Llanbister Road and Llandrindod Wells.	All Trains		55
Llandrindod Wells & Builth Road.	All Trains		45
Builth Road & Sugar Loaf Summit.	All Trains		50
Sugar Loaf Summit and Llandovery.	Passenger Trains		45
	Freight Trains		20
Llangadock	Over the Down Loop Line between 23m. 70c. and 23m. 53¼c.		15
Llangadock and Glanrhyd Halt	For heavy engines only		20
Llandilo, North End of Yard	Single Line	Double Line	15
Llandilo South	Double Line	Single Line	15
Carmarthen Valley Junction	Llandilo	Carmarthen	10
Ffairfach and Derwydd Road	Between 17¼ m.p. and 16m 30c.		20
,, ,, ,, ,,	Between 16m. 30c. and 15¼ m.p.		30
Derwydd Road	Through Station		15
Pantyffynnon North	All Down Trains between 10m. 38c. and 10m. 35c.		20
Pantyffynnon	Brynamman West Branch	Double Line	10
Pantyffynnon and Pontardulais	Between 9m. 5c. and 8m. 75c.		50
Pontardulais Junction	Llandovery	Swansea (Victoria)	15
Pontardulais and Gowerton South	All Trains		45
Through Gowerton Junction	All Trains		20
Gowerton South and Swansea (Victoria).	All Trains		35
Killay and Mumbles Road	Freight Trains		30
Swansea (Victoria) No. 2	Down Passenger Trains to come to dead stand at the junction at No. 2 Signal Box before proceeding into the Station.		

MAXIMUM SPEED OF TRAINS THROUGH JUNCTIONS AND OTHER SPECIFIED PLACES—continued.

Name of Place.	From	To	Miles per hour

PANTYFFYNNON AND BRYNAMMAN WEST.

The speed of all trains running between Pantyffynnon and Brynamman West in both directions must not exceed 30 miles per hour, except as shewn below :—

Pantyffynnon, to and from Llandovery Line.	All Trains		10
Pantyffynnon	Through connections 10m. 18c. and 10m. 21c.		10
Pontamman, through Tunnel between 11m. 55c. and 11m. 70c.	All Trains		15
Garnant, through Station	All Trains		15
Garnant and Brynamman West, between 15m. 70c. and 16m. 35c.	All Trains		15

GARNANT AND GWAUN-CAE-GURWEN.

Over Branch	All Trains		10

TIRYDAIL AND CROSS HANDS.

Freight Trains on this Branch must not exceed 15 miles per hour, and over the Curve between 1m. 5 ch. and 1m. 16ch. the speed must not exceed 5 miles per hour.

CARMARTHEN (Abergwili Jct.) AND LLANDILO (Carmarthen Valley Jct.).

Between Abergwili Junction and Carmarthen Valley Junction.	Except as otherwise shewn—All Up and Down Trains		50

PONTARDULAIS AND LLANELLY.

DOWN TRAINS.

Hendy Junction and Grovesend Colliery Loop Junction.	All Trains through Hendy Junction and over Loop between 0m. 25c. and 0m. 3c. between Llandovery Line and Swansea District Line		20
Hendy Junction and Morlais Junction.	Through Junctions and over Down Flying Loop		25
*Llangennech and Bynea	Between 2m. 65c. and 2¼ m.p.		40
,, ,, ,,	Between 2¼ m.p. and 1¾ m.p.		50
Llandilo Junction	Llandovery Line	Llanelly Dock	10
* ,, ,,	Llandovery Line	Main Line	40
Between Stop Lamps and over connections at St. David's Dock Crossing and over Llanelly Dock Junction—Morfa Junction Single Line			4
Morfa Junction	St. David's Line	Llanelly Dock Line	10
Llanelly Dock Level Crossing, North Side.	Over Level Crossing		5
Llanelly Dock	Llandilo Junction	Llanelly Dock Line	15
,, ,,	Llanelly Dock Loop		15

UP TRAINS.

Llanelly Dock	Llanelly Dock Loop		15
Llanelly Dock Level Crossing North Side.	Over Level Crossing		5
Morfa Junction	Llanelly Dock Line	St. David's Line	10
Between Stop Lamps and over connections at St. David's Dock Crossing and over Llanelly Dock Junction—Morfa Junction Single Line			4
Llandilo Junction	Main Line	Llandovery Line	40
,, ,,	Llanelly Dock	Llandovery Line	10
Bynea and Llangennech	1¾ to 2¼ m.p. all trains		50
* ,, ,,	2¼ m.p. to 2m. 65c. all trains		40
Morlais Junction	Llanelly	Pontardulais	40
Grovesend Colliery Loop Junction and Hendy Junction.	All Trains over Loop between 0m. 3c. and 0m. 25c., between Swansea District Line and Llandovery Line		20
Hendy Junction	Grovesend Colliery Loop Jct.	Pontardulais	20
Pontardulais	Single Line	Double Line	20

*—Permanent Restriction of Speed Indicator provided.

MAXIMUM LOADS FOR FREIGHT TRAINS WORKED BY L.M.R. ENGINES.

CRAVEN ARMS TO SWANSEA (VIC.).

SECTION.		MAXIMUM ENGINE LOADS.																											
		For Class 2 Engines.				For Class 3 Engines.				For Class 4 Engines.				For Class 5 Engines.				For Class 6 Engines.				For Class 7 Engines.				For Class 8 Engines.			
		CLASS OF TRAFFIC.																											
From	To	1	2	3	E.	1	2	3	E.	1	2	3	E.	1	2	3	E.	1	2	3	E.	1	2	3	E.	1	2	3	E.
Craven Arms	Broome	18	22	27	36	21	25	32	42	24	29	36	48	27	32	41	54	30	36	45	60	32	38	48	64	36	43	54	72
Broome	Hopton Heath	24	29	36	48	28	34	42	56	32	38	48	64	36	43	54	72	40	48	60	80	42	50	62	84	48	58	73	96
Hopton Heath	Bucknell	25	30	38	50	29	35	44	58	33	40	50	66	37	44	56	74	41	49	62	82	43	52	65	86	50	60	75	100
Bucknell	Knighton	22	26	33	44	25	30	38	50	29	35	44	58	33	40	50	60	36	43	54	72	38	46	57	76	44	53	66	88
Knighton	Llangunllo	14	17	21	28	16	19	24	32	18	22	27	36	21	25	32	42	23	28	35	46	24	29	36	48	28	34	42	56
Llangunllo	Llanbister Road ..	18	22	27	36	21	25	32	42	24	29	36	48	27	32	41	54	30	36	45	60	32	38	48	64	36	43	54	72
Llanbister Road ..	Penybont	30	36	45	60	30	36	45	60	35	42	53	70	45	54	68	90	45	54	68	90	50	60	75	100	50	60	75	100
Penybont	Llandrindod Wells ..	24	29	36	48	28	34	42	56	32	38	48	64	36	43	54	72	40	48	60	80	42	50	63	84	48	58	72	96
Llandrindod Wells ..	Howey	18	22	27	36	21	25	32	42	24	29	36	48	27	32	41	54	30	36	45	60	32	38	48	64	36	43	54	72
Howey	Builth Road	30	36	45	60	30	36	45	60	35	42	53	70	45	54	68	90	45	54	60	90	50	60	75	100	50	60	75	100
Builth Road	Llanwrtyd Wells ..	18	22	27	36	21	25	32	42	24	29	36	48	27	32	41	54	30	36	45	60	32	38	48	64	36	43	54	72
Llanwrtyd Wells ..	Sugar Loaf Summit ..	16	19	24	32	18	22	27	36	21	25	32	42	24	29	36	48	26	31	39	52	28	34	42	56	32	38	48	64
Sugar Loaf Summit ..	Llandovery	30	36	45	60	30	36	45	60	35	42	53	70	40	48	60	80	40	48	60	80	45	54	68	90	50	60	75	100
Llandovery	Llandilo	45	54	60	60	45	54	68	90	50	60	75	100	55	66	83	110	58	70	88	116	65	78	98	130	70	84	106	140
Llandilo	Derwydd Road	23	28	35	46	26	31	39	52	30	36	45	60	34	41	51	68	37	44	56	74	40	48	60	80	46	55	69	92
Derwydd Road	Pontardulais	35	42	53	70	35	42	53	70	40	48	60	80	45	54	68	90	50	60	75	100	55	66	83	110	60	72	90	120
Pontardulais	Grovesend	18	22	27	36	21	25	32	42	24	29	36	48	27	32	41	54	30	36	45	60	32	38	48	64	36	43	54	72
Grovesend	Glasbrook	35	42	53	70	35	42	53	70	40	48	60	80	45	54	68	90	50	60	75	100	50	60	75	100	60	72	90	120
Glasbrook	Dunvant	16	19	24	32	18	22	27	36	21	25	32	42	24	29	36	48	26	31	39	52	28	34	42	56	32	38	48	64
Dunvant	Mumbles Road	33	40	50	66	39	47	59	78	47	56	71	94	52	62	78	164	57	68	86	114	60	72	90	120	65	78	98	130
Mumbles Road	Swansea	18	22	27	36	21	25	32	42	24	29	36	48	27	32	41	54	30	36	45	60	33	40	50	66	36	43	54	72

STANDARD LOADS OF PASSENGER, PARCELS AND FISH TRAINS FOR ENGINE WORKING PURPOSES.

SECTION.		CLASS OF ENGINE.										
		L.M.R. Passenger Engines. Tons.						L.M.R. Freight Engines. Tons.				B.R. Engines. Tons.
From	To	Class 1. 2-4-0 2-4-2 T 0-4-4 T	Class 2. 4-4-0 2-4-2 T 0-4-4 T 0-6-2 T 2-6-2 T	Class 3. 4-4-0 2-4-2 T 2-6-2 T	Class 4. 4-4-0 4-6-0 2-6-4 T	Class 5. 4-6-0	Class 5X. 4-6-0	Class 2. 0-6-0 2-6-0 0-6-0T 0-6-2 T	Class 3. 0-6-0 0-6-0 T	Class 4. 0-6-0 4-6-0	Class 5. 2-6-0 4-6-0	Class 4. 4-6-0
LLANDILO AND CARMARTHEN.												
Carmarthen	Llandilo	210	285	340	380	435	495	315	375	420	475	380
Llandilo	Carmarthen	210	285	340	380	435	495	315	375	420	475	380
CRAVEN ARMS AND SWANSEA (Victoria).												
Swansea (Victoria)	Llandilo	145	195	235	260	300	340	220	260	290	330	260
Llandilo	Llandovery	210	285	340	380	435	495	315	375	420	475	380
Llandovery	Sugar Loaf Summit	110	150	180	200	230	260	165	200	220	250	200
Sugar Loaf Summit	Llandrindod Wells	145	195	235	260	300	340	220	260	290	330	260
Llandrindod Wells	Craven Arms	150	200	245	270	310	350	225	270	300	340	270
Craven Arms	Knighton	160	220	260	290	335	375	240	290	320	365	290
Knighton	Llangunllo	110	150	180	a200	230	260	165	200	220	250	a200
Llangunllo	Llandrindod Wells	160	220	260	290	335	375	240	290	320	365	290
Llandrindod Wells	Llandovery	145	195	235	260	300	340	220	260	290	330	260
Llandovery	Llandilo	210	285	340	380	435	495	315	375	420	475	380
Llandilo	Swansea (Victoria)	145	195	235	260	300	340	220	260	290	330	260

§—Excursion trains. a—210 tons when not stopping at Knucklas.

General Note.—In calculating the tonnage loading of passenger trains, loaded milk tanks must be counted as being of a total weight of 28 tons.

STATIONS.	K Freight.		E 5.20 a.m. Margam Sidings to Saltney Freight.		H 2.40 a.m. Swansea (Vic.) to Harlescott Sidings Freight.		J 7.5 a.m. Llandilo Junction to Glynhir Freight.		G Light Engine.	A Shrewsbury Passenger.		K Freight. RR MX		B Motor.	C 7.50 a.m. Llanelly Milk Empties.		A Shrewsbury Passenger.		G Light Engine.	E 5.20 a.m. Margam Sidings to Saltney Freight.		B 8.20 a.m. Llanelly Passenger.		K Limestone Freight.		B Pass.
	arr.	dep.	arr.	dep.	arr.	dep.	arr.	dep.	dep.	arr.	dep.	arr.	dep.	dep.	arr.	dep.	arr.	dep.	dep.	arr.	dep.	arr.	dep.	arr.	dep.	dep.
					M	X			SO	S	O															
	a.m.	a.m.	a.m.	a.m.	a.m.	a.m.	a.m.	a.m.	a.m.	a.m.	a.m.	a.m.	a.m.	a.m.	a.m.	a.m.	a.m.	a.m.	a.m.	a.m.	a.m.	a.m.	a.m.	a.m.	a.m.	a.m.
SWANSEA (Victoria)	—	6 30	..	..	..	..	..	..	7‖10	—	7 20	Z	..	7 20	..	..	—	7 55	..	..	..	..	..	..	..	..
Swansea Bay	—	—	..	..	..	..	..	..	—	—	7 24	..	..	7 24	..	..	—	7 59	..	..	..	..	..	..	..	..
Mumbles Road	—	—	..	..	..	..	..	..	—	—	7 29	..	..	7 29	..	..	—	8 4	..	..	..	..	..	..	..	..
Rhydydefed Siding	—	—	..	..	..	..	..	..	—	—	—	..	..	—	..	..	—	—	..	..	..	..	..	..	..	..
Killay	—	—	..	..	..	..	..	..	—	—	7 34	..	..	7 34	..	..	—	—	..	..	..	..	..	..	..	..
Dunvant	6	47	..	..	..	..	..	..	—	—	7 38	..	..	7 38	..	..	—	—	..	..	..	..	..	..	..	Am-
Gowerton South	6 57B	E7 2	..	..	..	..	..	..	—	7 41	7 43	..	..	7 43	..	..	—	—	..	..	..	..	..	..	..	man-
Glasbrook's Siding	—	—	..	..	..	..	..	..	—	—	—	..	..	—	..	..	—	—	..	..	..	..	..	..	..	ford
Gorseinon	7 10	—	..	..	..	..	..	..	7 28	—	7 48	..	..	7 48	..	..	—	—	..	..	..	..	..	..	..	arr.
Grovesend	..	..	..	..	..	..	..	..	—	—	—	..	..	—	..	..	—	—	..	..	..	..	..	..	..	8.58
Birch Rock Siding	..	..	..	..	..	..	..	..	—	—	—	..	..	—	..	..	—	—	..	..	..	..	..	..	..	a.m.
Cambria Siding	..	..	..	..	..	..	..	..	—	SUSPE	NDED	..	..	—	..	..	—	—	..	..	..	..	..	..	..	
Morlais Junction	..	..	..	..	..	..	7	21	SUS-	..	..	..	..	..	8	2	..	..	..	..	..	8	33	..	..	SUS-
Hendy Junction	..	..	6	48	..	..	—	—	PEN	..	..	..	..	..	—	—	..	..	..	..	..	—	—	..	..	PEN-
Hendy Siding	..	..	—	—	..	..	—	—	DED	..	..	..	..	..	—	—	..	..	..	..	..	—	—	..	..	DED
PONTARDULAIS	..	..	6 52*	7 0	..	..	7 37	8 55	7‖38	—	7 57	..	..	7 56	8	6	8 21	8 22	..	..	..	8 35	8 38	..	..	..
Glynhir	..	..	—	—	..	..	..	..	..	—	—	..	..	..	—	—	—	—	..	..	..	—	—	..	..	..
PANTYFFYNNON	..	..	7 13X	7 24	..	..	See		26th July	—	8 5	..	..	..	8 13	8 16	8 29	8 30	..	..	..	8 45	8 48	..	..	8 55
Ammanford	..	..	..	..	..	..	page 144.		to	Runs SO		..	..	..	..	..	Y—Calls at		..	..	..	..	..	..	..	9 1
Ammanford Coll. Halt	..	..	..	..	..	..	..	..	30th	26th July		..	..	..	..	..	Garth to		..	..	..	..	..	..	..	9 3
Glanamman	..	..	..	..	..	..	..	..	Aug.	to		..	..	..	..	..	pick up		..	..	..	..	..	..	..	9 9
Gellyceidrim Coll. Sdg	..	..	..	..	..	..	..	..	(incl.).	30th Aug.		..	..	..	..	..	passengers		..	..	..	..	..	..	..	—
GARNANT	..	..	..	..	..	..	..	..	..	(inclusive).		..	..	..	..	..	for beyond		..	..	..	..	..	..	..	9 13
Gwaun-cae-GurwenC.	..	..	..	..	..	..	..	..	..	..	..	..	..	..	..	..	Shrewsbury on notice		..	..	..	..	..	..	..	..
BRYNAMMAN WEST	..	..	..	..	..	..	..	..	..	..	..	..	..	..	..	..	being given previous day.		..	..	..	..	..	..	..	9 18
Pantyffynnon North	B	..	—	—	..	..	..	..	..	—	—	..	..	..	—	—	V—Two minutes		..	..	..	—	—	—	9 0	..
Parcyrhun Halt		..	—	—	..	..	..	..	..	—	—	..	..	..	—	—	recovery time		..	..	..	—	8 51½	—	—	..
Tirydail	Pass.	..	7	29	..	..	..	..	..	—	—	..	..	..	—	—	Knighton to		..	..	..	8 54	8 57	—	—	..
Llandebie		..	7 35X	CT7 41	..	..	..	..	..	—	—	..	..	..	—	—	Craven Arms.		..	..	..	—	9 3	9 11X	9 45	..
Cilyrychen Crossing	dep.	..	—	—	..	..	..	..	..	—	—	..	..	..	—	—			..	..	..	—	—	—	—	..
Derwydd Road		..	7 51X	7 55	..	..	..	..	..	8	15	..	..	..	8 29*	8 45	8	X39	..	..	..	9 4	9 7	9 56X	10 17	..
Ffairfach	a.m.	..	—	—	..	..	..	..	..	—	—	..	..	..	8 52	—	—	—	..	..	..	9 11½	9 14	..	..	..
CARMARTHEN	7 0	..	..	..	..	..	..	..	..	..	..	..	..	..	..	..	..	..	..	..	..	..	..	..	..	..
Abergwili Junction	7 4	..	..	..	..	..	..	..	..	..	..	..	..	..	..	..	..	..	..	..	..	..	..	..	..	..
Abergwili	7 6½	..	..	..	..	..	..	..	..	..	..	..	..	..	..	..	..	..	..	..	..	..	..	..	..	..
Nantgaredig	7 14	..	..	..	..	..	..	..	..	..	..	..	..	..	..	..	..	..	..	..	..	..	..	..	..	..
Llanarthney	7 19	..	..	..	..	..	..	..	..	..	..	..	..	..	..	..	..	..	..	..	..	..	..	..	..	..
Drysllwyn	7 24	..	..	..	..	..	..	..	..	..	..	..	..	..	..	..	..	..	..	..	..	..	..	..	..	..
Golden Grove	7.30	..	..	..	..	..	..	..	..	..	..	..	..	..	..	..	..	..	..	..	..	..	..	..	..	..
Llandilo Bridge	7 38	..	..	..	..	..	..	..	..	..	..	..	..	..	..	..	..	..	..	..	..	..	..	..	..	..
Carmarthen Valley Jct.	7 40	..	8	7	..	..	..	..	..	8	21	..	..	..	..	..	8	45	..	See		9	15	..	..	..
LLANDILO	7 42	..	8	9	..	..	..	..	..	—	8 24	..	..	..	..	..	8 47	8 48	..	page 142.		9 17X	9 19	..	..	..
Talley Road Halt	..	..	—	—	..	..	..	..	..	—	—	..	..	..	..	..	—	—	..	..	..	9 23	9 23½	..	..	..
Glanrhyd Halt	..	..	—	—	..	..	..	..	..	—	—	..	..	..	..	..	—	—	..	..	..	—	9 28½	..	..	..
Llangadock	..	..	8	24	..	..	..	..	..	8	33	..	..	..	..	..	8 57X	8 59	..	..	..	9 31½	X9 32½	..	..	..
Llanwrda	..	..	8	31	..	..	..	..	..	8	36	..	..	..	..	..	—	9 3	..	..	..	9 36½	9 38	..	..	..
LLANDOVERY	..	..	842EO	BE925	..	..	..	..	..	8 42X	8 46	..	..	..	..	..	9 9X	9 13	..	842EO	BE925	9 45X	—	..	..	..
Cynghordy	..	..	..	..	..	..	..	..	..	8	55	..	..	..	..	..	9	23	After	9 43X	9 53	..	..	..	..	..
Sugar Loaf Summit	..	..	..	..	..	..	..	..	..	9	4	..	..	..	..	..	9	33	bank-	10 13X	P10 18	..	..	..	..	..
Llanwrtyd Wells	..	..	See		..	..	..	..	..	9	8	..	..	..	..	..	9 37X	9 38	ing	10 27X	P10 32	..	..	..	..	..
Llangammarch Wells	..	..	page 143.		..	..	..	..	..	—	—	..	..	..	..	..	—	9 43	9.25	—	—	..	..	..	..	..
Garth	..	..	..	..	..	..	..	..	..	9 16X	9 19	..	..	..	K		—	9Y48	a.m.	10	42	..	..	..	..	..
Cilmery Halt	..	..	..	..	..	..	..	..	..	—	—	..	..	..			—	—	Shrew-	—	—	..	..	..	..	..
BUILTH ROAD (H.L.) ↞	..	..	..	..	..	..	..	..	..	9 29	9 33	..	..	..			9 56	9 59	sbury	1057B	E11 2	..	..	..	..	..
Howey	..	..	..	..	See		..	..	..	9	39	..	..	..	Freight.		10	5	to	11	15	..	..	..	..	..
LLANDRINDOD WELLS	..	..	..	..	page 140.		..	..	..	9 44	9 46	..	..	..			10 10	10 11	Swan-	11	23	..	..	..	..	..
Penybont	..	..	..	..	..	..	..	..	..	9	51	..	..	..	RR	MO	—	10 17	sea	11	32	..	..	..	..	..
Penybont Junction	..	..	..	..	..	..	..	..	..	9	53	..	..	..			10	20	(Vic.).	11	34	..	..	..	..	..
Dolau	..	..	..	..	..	..	..	..	..	—	—	..	..	..	arr.	dep.	—	—	..	11 42C	G1145	..	..	..	..	..
Llanbister Road	..	..	..	..	..	..	..	..	..	10	2	..	..	..			10	27	..	11	56	..	..	..	..	..
Llangunllo	..	..	..	..	9 12P	*9 42	..	..	..	10	6	..	..	..	a.m.	a.m.	10	31	11‖52	12 7	P1212	..	..	..	..	..
Knucklas	..	..	..	..	—	BE	..	..	..	—	—	..	..	..	Z	..	—	—	p.m.	—	—	..	..	..	..	..
KNIGHTON	..	..	..	..	1070W	P1012	..	..	..	10 16	10 21	—	10 5	..	—	10 25	10 41	10 44	12‖ 4	1237O	W1*20	..	..	..	..	..
Bucknell	..	..	..	..	—	—	..	..	..	—	—	10 15	10 35	..	10 35	10 55	—	—	..	..	..	..	..	..	..	..
Hopton Heath	..	..	..	..	—	—	..	..	..	—	—	10 45	11 5	..	11 5	11 25	V	—	..	See		..	..	..	..	..
Broome	..	..	..	..	—	—	..	..	..	—	—	11 13	11 33	..	11 33	11 53	—	—	..	page 146.		..	..	..	..	..
CRAVEN ARMS	..	..	..	..	10 42*	11 25	..	..	..	10 40	10 44	11 41	—	..	12 1	—	11 0	11 2	..	..	..	..	..	..	..	..
Shrewsbury	..	..	..	..	1§10	—	..	..	..	11 16	—	..	..	..	..	..	11 33	—	..	..	..	..	..	..	..	..

Z—Worked by Knighton Bank Engine after assisting 5.17 a.m. Coleham.

	F		G	G	H		G	G	G		G	H	
STATIONS.	9.40 p.m. Coleham Freight.		Light Engine.	Light Engine.	7.15 p.m. Stafford Freight.		Light Engine.	Light Engine.	Light Engine.		Light Engine.	9.45 p.m. (Suns.) Crewe to Swansea Freight.	
	arr.	dep.	dep.	dep.	arr.	dep.	dep.	dep.	arr.	dep.	arr.	arr.	dep.
			MX		M	X	MX	MX	M	X	MX	M	O
	p.m.	p.m.	a.m.	a.m.	a.m.	a.m.	a.m.	a.m.	a.m.	a.m.	a.m.	p.m.	a.m.
Shrewsbury	..	..	..	..	..	..	..	..	..	..	..	1135E	TY12 40
CRAVEN ARMS	..	..	..	..	..	..	..	..	..	..	..	1 43O	W2 5
Broome	..	..	..	..	..	..	..	..	..	..	..	—	—
Hopton Heath	See		..	..	See		..	..	..	..	..	Y—Cole-	
Bucknell	page	135.	..	..	page	135.	After	..	..	..	..	ham.	
KNIGHTON	..	..	..	..	12 19X	12 40	bank-	..	—	2‖25	..	2 40	3 0
Knucklas	..	..	..	..	—	—	ing	..	—	—	..	—	—
Llangunllo	11 42X	11N43	..	..	1 10		8.55	1‖35	2‖50X	2‖51	..	3 30	
Llanbister Road	11 52X	11 53	..	..	1 18C	T1 23	p.m.	1 41	2 57		..	3 38	
Dolau	M	X	..	..	—	—	Swan-	—	—	—	..	—	—
Penybont Junction	12 8		..	..	1 34		sea.	1 50	3 9		..	3 49	
Penybont	12 10		..	..	1 36		(Vic.)	1 52	3 11		..	3 51	
LLANDRINDOD WELLS	12 18		..	..	1 44			2X13	3‖20X	3‖32	..	3 59	
Howey	12 25		..	..	1 56X	2 5	2‖26	2‖26	3 38		..	4 9	
BUILTH ROAD (H.L.) ←«	1234O	W1239	..	..	2 15O	W2 25	2‖35	2‖35	3 45	—	..	4 19	4 40
Cilmery Halt	M	X	..	..	—	—	..	..			..		
Garth	12 53		..	..	2 42X	2 45	..	..	To Bank		..		
Llangammarch Wells	—	—	..	..	—	—	..		12.15 a.m.		..	See	
Llanwrtyd Wells	1X 7		..	..	3 X1		..	After	Swansea		..	page 121.	
Sugar Loaf Summit	1 21P	X1 27	3 ‖ 4	..	3 16X	P3 32	..	assist-	(Vic.)		4‖X25		
Cynghordy	1X 39		3 12	..	3 47	X4 0	..	ing	Freight.		4 33	..	..
LLANDOVERY	1 55E	T2 30	3‖21	..	4 14E	T4X40	..	6.45	..	..	4‖X42	..	..
Llanwrda	2 39			..	4 51		..	p.m.	..	..	..	..	..
Llangadock	2 44		..	..	4 57C	T5X0	..	Swan-	..	..	..	..	..
Glanrhyd Halt	—	—	..	..	—	—	..	sea.	..	..	..	..	..
Talley Road Halt	—	—	..	..	—	—	..	(Vic).	..	..	..	..	..
LLANDILO	2 57C	T3 25	..	..	5 14	5 24	..		..	..	..	..	..
Carmarthen Valley Jct.	3 28		..	..	5 27		..	2.26	..	..	..	..	..
Llandilo Bridge	N—11 43		..	..	..	..	..	a.m. Light	..	..	..	..	..
Golden Grove	p.m. MX		..	..	..	..	..	Engine	..	..	..	..	..
Dryslwyn	Light Engine		..	..	..	..	..	Howey	..	..	..	..	..
Llanarthney	Llangunllo		..	..	..	..	..	to	..	..	..	..	..
Nantgaredig	to Builth		..	..	..	..	..	Builth	..	..	..	..	..
Abergwili	Road to run		..	..	..	..	..	Road.	..	..	..	..	..
Abergwili Jct.	attached.		..	..	..	..	..	at-	..	..	..	..	..
CARMARTHEN			..	..	..	..	..	tached	..	..	..	..	..
Ffairfach	3 30		..	..	5 29		..	..	..	..	..	..	..
Derwydd Road	3 38		..	..	5 38		..	..	..	..	..	..	..
Cilyrychen Crossing	—	—	..	..	—	—	..	..	..	..	..	..	..
Llandebie	3 44		..	..	5 44		..	..	..	..	..	..	..
Tirydail	3 49		..	..	5 49		..	..	..	..	..	..	..
Parcyrhun Halt	—	—	..	..	—	—	..	..	..	..	..	..	..
Pantyffynnon North	—	—	..	..	—	—	..	..	..	..	..	..	..
BRYNAMMAN WEST	..	..	..	..	..	..	..	..	..	..	H	..	..
Stop Board	..	..	..	..	..	..	..	..	..	..	Severn	..	..
Gwaun-cae-Gurwen C.	..	..	..	..	..	..	..	..	..	..	Tunnel	..	..
Stop Board No. 1	..	..	..	..	..	..	..	..	..	..	Jct.	..	..
Stop Board No. 2	..	..	..	..	..	..	..	..	..	..	Freight	..	..
Stop Board No. 3	..	..	..	..	..	..	..	..	..	..		..	..
GARNANT	..	..	..	..	..	..	..	..	..	..	dep.	..	..
Glanamman	..	..	..	..	..	..	..	..	..	..		..	..
Stop Board	..	..	..	..	..	..	..	..	..	..	a.m.	..	..
Ammanford Coll. Halt	..	..	..	..	..	..	..	..	..	..	..	..	..
Ammanford	..	..	..	..	..	..	..	..	..	..	..	..	..
PANTYFFYNNON	3 53		K	..	5 53		..	..	..	..	6 55	..	..
Glynhir	—	—		..	—	—	..	..	..	..	—	..	..
PONTARDULAIS	4 4	4 20	Beach	..	6 6	6 40	..	..	..	..	7 6	..	..
Hendy Siding	..	..	Sidings to	..	..	..	..	..	..	..	—	..	..
Hendy Junction	..	..	Goods	..	..	..	..	..	..	..	7 9	..	..
Morlais Junction	..	..	Yard Freight	..	..	..	..	..	..	..		..	..
Cambria Siding	—	—		..	—	—	..	..	..	..	..	..	..
Grovesend	—	—	dep.	..	—	—	..	..	..	..	..	..	..
Gorseinon	4 31	4 46		..	6 55	7 10	..	..	..	..	..	..	..
Glasbrook's Siding	—	—		..	—	—	..	..	..	..	..	..	..
Gowerton South	4 51		a.m.	7‖5	7 15		..	..	..	..	..	..	..
Dunvant	—	—	..	7 10	7 25		..	..	..	..	..	..	..
Killay	—	—	..	—	—	—	..	..	..	..	..	..	..
Rhydydefed Siding	—	—	..	—	—	—	..	..	..	..	..	..	..
Mumbles Road	—	—	..	—	—	—	..	..	..	..	..	..	..
Swansea Bay	—	—	..	—	—	—	..	..	..	..	..	..	..
SWANSEA (Victoria)	5 11	—	6 45	7‖25	7 40	—	..	..	..	..	..	..	..

	H		E		H		G		G	B		B	B
STATIONS.	Freight.		10.58 p.m. SX Crewe Vacuum Freight.		9.45 p.m. (Sundays) Crewe to Swansea Freight.		Light Engine.		Light Engine.	9.50 p.m. SX 9.50 p.m. (Suns.) York Passenger and Mail.		Pass.	Motor.
	arr.	dep.	arr.	dep.	arr.	dep.	arr.	dep.	dep.	arr.	dep.	dep.	dep.
	M	O	M	X	M	O	M	X	MX				
	a.m.	a.m.	a.m.	a.m.	a.m.	a.m.	a.m.	a.m.	a.m.	a.m.	a.m.	a.m.	a.m.
Shrewsbury	..	..	1 8O	W1 18	..	..	..	..	..	—	3 45	..	..
CRAVEN ARMS	..	..	2 40		..	..	..	..	After	4 17	4 22	..	..
Broome	..	..	—	—	..	..	..	..	bank-	—	—	..	..
Hopton Heath	..	..	—	—	..	..	..	..	ing	—	—	..	..
Bucknell	..	..	—	—	..	..	..	..	12.15	—	4 36	..	..
KNIGHTON	..	..	3 10O	W3 17	..	..	..	..	a.m.	4 42	4 50	..	..
Knucklas	..	..	—	—			..	..	Swan-	—	—	..	..
Llangunllo	..	..	3 45C	D3 50	See		—	4 15	sea	5 2		..	..
Llanbister Road	..	..	3 58	4X1	page 120.		4 21		(Vic.)	5 7		..	..
Dolau	..	..	—	—			—	—	to	—	—	..	..
Penybont Junction	..	..	4 16		..	..	4 31		Shrew-	5 15		..	..
Penybont	..	..	4 18		..	..	4 33		sbury.	5 17		..	..
LLANDRINDOD WELLS	..	..	4 X26		..	..	4X 41			5 22	5 27	..	..
Howey	..	..	4 38		..	..	4‖48	4‖50	4‖50	5 32		..	..
BUILTH ROAD (H.L.) ←«	..	..	4 41		4 19	4 40	4‖58	—	4‖58	5 37	5 41	..	..
Cilmery Halt	..	..	—	—	—	—				—	—	..	..
Garth	..	..	4 55		4 55		After		At-	—	5Z50	..	..
Llangammarch Wells	..	..	—	—	—	—	assisting		tached	—	5Z56	..	..
Llanwrtyd Wells	..	..	5 X8		5 10		9.45 p.m.		to	6 2	6 3	..	..
Sugar Loaf Summit	..	..	5 22P	5 25	5 26P	5 34	Swansea		4.15	6 10		..	..
Cynghordy	..	..	5 X38		5 49		(Victoria)		a.m.	6X 17		..	..
LLANDOVERY	—	5 55	5 54E	W6X0	6 2XE	T6 39	Freight.		Light	6 24	6 32	..	..
Llanwrda	6 6		6 9						En-	6 38	6 40	..	..
Llangadock	6 12		6 14		See		..	..	gine	6 43X	6 48	..	..
Glanrhyd Halt	—	—	—	—	page 122.		..	..	ex	—	—	..	..
Talley Road Halt	—	—	—	—			..	..	Llan-	—	—	..	..
LLANDILO	6 26X	6 41	6 28X	6 45	..	..	..	..	gullo.	6 57	7 5	..	..
Carmarthen Valley Jct.	6 44		6 48		..	..	..	..		7 7		..	..
Llandilo Bridge	..	..	..	..	..	..	..	..	..	..	..	..	..
Golden Grove	..	..	..	..	..	..	..	..	..	..	..	..	..
Dryslwyn	..	..	..	..	..	..	..	..	..	..	..	..	..
Llanarthney	..	..	..	..	..	..	..	..	..	..	..	..	..
Nantgaredig	..	..	..	..	..	..	..	..	..	..	..	..	..
Abergwili	..	..	..	..	..	..	..	..	..	..	..	..	..
Abergwili Jct.	..	..	..	..	..	..	..	..	..	..	..	..	..
CARMARTHEN	..	..	..	..	..	..	..	..	..	..	..	..	..
Ffairfach	6 46		6 50		..	..	..	..	..	—	—	..	..
Derwydd Road	6 55		6 58		..	..	..	..	..	7 13X	7 14	..	..
Cilyrychen Crossing	—	—	—	—	..	..	..	..	..	—	—	..	..
Llandebie	7 2X	7 25	7 5X	*7 38	..	..	..	..	..	—	—	..	..
Tirydail	7 31		7 44		..	..	..	..	..	—	—	..	..
Parcyrhun Halt	—	—	—	—	..	..	..	..	..	—	—	..	..
Pantyffynnon North	—	—	—	—	..	..	..	..	..	—	—	..	..
BRYNAMMAN WEST	..	..	..	..	..	..	..	..	..	Z—Stops at		7 45	..
Stop Board	..	..	..	..	..	..	..	..	..	Garth to set down		—	..
Gwaun-cae-Gurwen C.	..	..	..	..	..	..	..	..	..	newspaper		SUS-	..
Stop Board No. 1	..	..	..	..	..	..	..	..	..	traffic only,		PEN-	..
Stop Board No. 2	..	..	..	..	..	..	..	..	..	and at		DED	..
Stop Board No. 3	..	..	..	..	..	..	..	..	..	Llangam- march Wells		..	..
GARNANT	..	..	..	..	..	..	..	..	..	for		7 51	..
Glanamman	..	..	..	..	..	..	..	..	..	Post Office		7 54	..
Stop Board	..	..	..	..	..	..	..	..	..	purposes and		—	..
Ammanford Coll. Halt	..	..	..	..	..	..	..	..	..	to take up		8 0	..
Ammanford	..	..	..	..	..	..	..	..	..	as required.		8 2	..
PANTYFFYNNON	7 35		7 48		..	..	..	..	..	7 23	7 26	8 5	..
Glynhir	—	—	—	—	..	..	..	..	..	—	—		..
PONTARDULAIS	7 48	8 25	7 59	8 25	..	..	..	..	..	7 33	7 35	..	8 18
Hendy Siding	..	..	..	..	..	..	..	..	..	..	..	..	..
Hendy Junction	..	..	..	..	..	..	..	..	..	..	..	..	..
Morlais Junction	..	..	..	..	..	..	..	..	..	..	..	..	..
Cambria Siding	—	—	—	—	..	..	..	..	..	—	—	..	—
Grovesend	—	—	—	—	..	..	..	..	..	—	—	..	—
Gorseinon	8 38	8 55	—	—	..	..	..	..	..	7 41	7 43	..	8 25
Glasbrook's Siding	—	—	—	—	..	..	..	..	..	—	—	..	—
Gowerton South	9 1		8 43		..	..	..	..	..	—	—	..	8 29
Dunvant	9 6		8 51		..	..	..	..	..	—	—	..	8 32½
Killay	—	—	—	—	..	..	..	..	..	—	—	..	8 36
Rhydydefed Siding	—	—	—	—	..	..	..	..	..	—	—	..	—
Mumbles Road	—	—	—	—	..	..	..	..	..	—	—	..	8 40
Swansea Bay	—	—	—	—	..	..	..	..	..	7 59	8 0	..	8 44½
SWANSEA (Victoria)	9 23	—	9 5	—	..	..	..	..	..	8 4	—	..	8 48½

STATIONS.	G		B		B			B		K		K		G	B		K		K		K	B	B	B		B
	Engine and Van. MO RR		Passenger.		Passenger.			Pass.		Return 9.15 a.m. Pantyffynnon Freight.		Swansea Freight.		Light Engine.	Passenger. SO		9.0 a.m. Craven Arms to Llandovery Freight.		4.0 p.m. Pontardulais Freight.		Return Mountain Freight	Pass.	Pass. SX	Llanelly Passenger.		Motor.
	dep.		arr.	dep.	arr	dep.		dep.		arr.	dep.	arr.	dep.	dep.	arr.	dep.	arr.	dep.	arr.	dep.	dep.	dep.	dep	arr.	dep.	dep.
Shrewsbury	p.m.		SO a.m. —	a.m. 11§57	p.m. —	p.m. 12‡ 5		SO p.m.		a.m. —	p.m.	p.m.	p.m.	SO p.m.	p.m. —	p.m. 12 30	p.m.	p.m.	p.m.	p.m.	SX p.m.	SO p.m.	p.m.	p.m.	p.m.	p.m.
CRAVEN ARMS	12†20		12 32	12 34	**12 43**	**12‡52**									1 8	1 15										
Broome	—		—	—	—	—									—	—										
Hopton Heath	—		—V	—	—	—									—	—										
Bucknell	—		—	12 58	—	1 6									—	1 32										
KNIGHTON	12†50		1 4X	1 11	**1 12X**	**1 15**									1 38	1 42										
Knucklas			—	—	—	—									—	—							Sats. and School Holidays excepted.			
Llangunllo	After working 10.25 a.m. MO RR ex Knighton.		1	24	—	1 29									—	1 59										
Llanbister Road			1	27	—	1 34									—	2 5										
Dolau			—	—	—	1 39									—	2 11										
Penybont Junction			1	35	C1	43S									2	15	See page 127.									
Penybont			1	37	—	1 46									—	2 18										
LLANDRINDOD WELLS			1 42	1 43	—	**1 52**									2 23X	2 27										
Howey			1	48	C1	57S									2	X32										
BUILTH ROAD (H.L.) ←«			1 53	1 56	**2 2**	**2 5**									2 37X	2 43	**1 54**	**2 55**								
Cilmery Halt			—	—	—	—									—	—	—	—								
Garth			—	2 X4	—	2 13									—	2 52	**3 10**	**3 30**								
Llangammarch Wells			—	2 9	—	2 18									—	2 57	—	—								
Llanwrtyd Wells			2 15X	2 20	2 24	X2 26									—	3 4	**3 45**	**X5 0**								
Sugar Loaf Summit			2	27	2	33V									3	11										
Cynghordy			2	33	—	2 40									—	3 18								**SUSPE**	**NDED**	
LLANDOVERY			2 40	2 46	**2 47**	**2 52**									3 25X	3 30	See page 130.					**SUS-PEN-DED**	**4 10**	—	**4 10**	
Llanwrda			—	2 54	—	2 59									3 36X	3 37							4 18	—	4 18	
Llangadock			—	3 0	—	3 3									—	3 41							4 21	—	4 23	
Glanrhyd Halt			—	—	—	—									—	—								4 26½	4 27	
Talley Road Halt			—	—	—	—									—	—								4 31½	4 32	
LLANDILO			3 10	3 14	**3 14**	**X3 18**		3 25							3 50	3 53						4 20		**4 36**	**4 37½**	
Carmarthen Valley Jct.			3	16	3	20		3 27							3	55						4 22		4	39½	
Llandilo Bridge			**SUSPENDED** Runs **SO** 19th July to 30th August inclusive.		**V**—Stops at Sugar Loaf Summit if required **FX**, and on Fridays only to take up market passengers.			3 30														4 25				
Golden Grove								3 35														4 30				
Dryslwyn								3 40							**SUSPE**	**NDED**						4 35				
Llanarthney								3 45														4 40				
Nantgaredig								3 53														4 48				
Abergwili								3 59														4 54	**B**			
Abergwili Jct.								4 1														4 56				
CARMARTHEN								4 5														5 0				
Ffairfach			—	—	—	—									—	—							Llanelly Pass.	4 40½	4 41	
Derwydd Road			3	21	3	27									4	2								4 48	4 48½	
Cilyrychen Crossing			—	—	—	—									—	—								—	—	
Llandebie			—	—	—	—									—	—								4 51½	4 52	
Tirydail	K		—	3 28	—	3 34									—	4 9					4 30		dep.	4 55½	4 56	
Parcyrhun Halt			—	—	—	—									—	—					—		p.m.	—	4 59	
Pantyffynnon North			—	—	—	—									—	—					—			—	—	
BRYNAMMAN WEST	Return 5.45 a.m. Llandilo Jct. **Freight.** Third Trip.		§—Advertised Shrewsbury depart 11.55 a.m.		‡—Advertised Shrewsbury depart 12.0 noon. Craven Arms depart 12.50 p.m.					11 25	12 5												**4 35**			
Stop Board										**P**	—												—			
Gwaun-cae-Gurwen C.								**B**																		
Stop Board No. 1	arr.	dep.															**K**									
Stop Board No. 2																										
Stop Board No. 3	p.m.	p.m.	**V**—Seven minutes recovery time.					Motor.		p.m.																Ordinary engine and coaches on Saturdays.
GARNANT										12 19	12 30						Return 2.35 p.m. Llandilo Jct. **Freight.**						**4 41**			
Glanamman								dep.		12 40	●2 30												4 44			
Stop Board										2 38	P2 41												—			
Ammanford Coll. Halt	See page 127.							**SX** p.m.		2 47	X3 45												4 50			
Ammanford										—	—						arr.	dep.					4 52			
PANTYFFYNNON	—	—	3	32	—	**3 39**				**3 53**	—				4 13	4 14	p.m.	p.m.			**4 36**		**4 57**	**5 1**	**5 4**	
Glynhir	—	—	—	—	—	—									—	—	**4 30**	**4 45**					—	—	—	
PONTARDULAIS	**2 54 ●**	**3 35**	3 39	3 41	**3 46**	**3 48**		**3 53**				—	**4 0**		4 21	4 23	**4 49**	**6 15**					**5 5**	**5 11**	**5 12**	**5 20**
Hendy Siding	3	39						**SUS-PEN-DED**									**6 19**	**7 0**	See page 128.				—	—	—	
Hendy Junction	—	—															—	—					—	—	—	
Morlais Junction	3L	43															7	8					5 8½	5	15½	
Cambria Siding			—	—	—	—		—				—	—		—	—			—	—						—
Grovesend			—	—	—	—		—				—	—		—	—			—	—						—
Gorseinon			—	3 48	—	3 55		4 0				**4 15 ●**	**4 35**	4‖25	4 29	4 30			4 15 ●	4 35						5 27
Glasbrook's Siding			—	—	—	—		—						—	—	—			—	—						—
Gowerton South			3 51	3 53	—	3 59		4 5						—	4 33	4 34			4 45	4 55						5 31
Dunvant			—	—	—	—		4 9						—	—	—			5	5						5 36
Killay			—	—	—	—		4 13						—	—	—			—	—						5 41
Rhydydefed Siding			—	—	—	—		—						—	—	—			—	—						—
Mumbles Road			—	4 3	—	4 9		4 19				see page 129.		—	—	4 44			—	—						5 46
Swansea Bay			—	4 8	—	4 14		4 24						—	4 48	4 49			—	—						5 51
SWANSEA (Victoria)			4 12	—	**4 18**	—		**4 28**						4‖50	4 53	—			5 20	—						5 55

STATIONS.	B Shrewsbury Passenger. arr.	dep.	H 11.15 a.m. Llandilo Junction to Shrewsbury Freight. arr.	dep.	K Moun-tain Freight. dep.	K Freight. arr.	dep.	B Motor. SO dep.	H Llandovery Freight. arr.	dep.	B Motor. dep.	K 10.10 a.m. Llandovery Freight. arr.	dep.	K 9.30 a.m. Llandilo Junction Freight. arr.	dep.	H 11.15 a.m. Llandilo Junction to Shrewsbury Freight. arr.	dep.	B 2.25 p.m. Llanelly Passenger. arr.	dep.	H 1.15 p.m. Swansea (Vic.) to Llandovery Sidings Freight. arr.	dep.	B 2.50 p.m. Llanelly to Brynamman West Passenger. arr.	dep.	B Pass. dep.	K 12.40 p.m. Pantyffynnon Freight. 2nd Trip arr.	dep.
					SX				M	X										M	X	S	O		S	X
	p.m.	p.m.	a.m.	p.m.	p.m.	p.m.	p.m.	p.m.	p.m.	p.m.	p.m.	p.m.	p.m.	p.m.	p.m.	p.m.	p.m.	p.m.	p.m.	p.m.	p.m.	p.m.	p.m.	p.m.	p.m.	p.m.
SWANSEA (Victoria)	—	**12 25**	..	..	..	..	..	*1 5*	—	1 15	**1 35**	..	..	..	..	..	..	..	..	..	..	..	..	..	..	..
Swansea Bay	—	12 29	..	..	..	..	..	*1 9*	—	—	1 39	..	..	..	..	..	..	..	..	..	..	..	..	..	..	..
Mumbles Road	—	12 34	..	..	..	..	..	*1 14*	—	—	1 44	..	..	..	..	..	..	..	..	..	..	..	..	..	..	..
Rhydydefed Siding	—	—	..	..	..	..	..	—	—	—	—	..	..	..	..	..	..	..	..	..	..	..	..	..	..	..
Killay	—	—	..	..	..	..	..	*1 19*	—	—	1 49	..	..	..	..	..	..	..	..	..	..	..	..	..	..	..
Dunvant	—	—	..	..	..	..	..	*1 22*	—	—	1 52	..	..	..	..	..	..	..	..	..	..	..	..	..	..	..
Gowerton South	12 43	12 45	..	..	..	**12 17**	**1 10**	*1 27*	—	—	1 57	..	..	..	..	..	..	**SUSPE**	**NDED**	..	..	..	..	..	..	..
Glasbrook's Siding	—	—	..	..	..	**1 15**	**1 40**	—	—	—	—	..	..	..	..	..	..	..	..	..	..	..	..	..	..	..
Gorseinon	—	—	..	..	..	**1 45**	**2Z35**	*1 32*	—	—	2 2	..	..	..	..	..	..	..	..	..	..	..	..	..	..	..
Grovesend	12 48	12 50	..	..	..			—	—	—	—	..	..	..	..	..	..	..	..	..	..	..	..	..	..	..
Birch Rock Siding	—	—	..	..	..			—	—	—	—	..	..	..	..	..	..	..	..	..	..	..	..	..	..	..
Cambria Siding	—	—	..	..	..	**Z**—Ten minutes later on Saturdays.		—	—	—	—	..	..	..	..	..	..	..	..	..	..	..	..	..	..	..
Morlais Junction	..	..	See page 147.		..			..	..	..	**SUS-PEN-DED**	..	..	..	..	..	..	2 37½		..	..	3 4		..	..	..
Hendy Junction	..	..			..			..	..	..		..	..	..	..	..	..	—	—	..	..	—	—	..	..	..
Hendy Siding	..	..			..			..	..	..		..	..	..	..	..	..	—	—	..	..	—	—	..	..	..
PONTARDULAIS	**12 58**	**12 59**	11 37	12 0	..	..	..	*1 40*	1 57	2 30	**2 10**	..	..	..	..	..	..	**2 40½**	**2 41½**	..	..	*3 7*	*3 9*	..	..	..
Glynhir	—	—	—	—	..	..	..		—	—		..	..	..	..	..	..	—	—	..	..	—	—	..	..	..
PANTYFFYNNON	**1 6**	**1 7**	12 10*	12 50	**1 10**	..	..	..	2 43		..	..	..	..	..	..	..	**2 48½**	**2 50½**	..	..	*3 17*	*3 25*	**3 25**	3 12	**4 15**
Ammanford	**N**—Calls on Thursdays only to set down cash safe.		..	..	..	..	..	..	..	..	..	..	..	..	..	..	..	..	..	..	..	Works 3.25 p.m. Pantyffynnon to Brynamman West on Saturdays.		3 29	—	—
Ammanford Coll. Halt			..	..	..	..	..	..	..	..	..	..	..	..	..	..	..	..	..	..	..			3X31	—	—
Glanamman			..	..	..	..	..	..	..	..	..	..	..	..	..	..	..	..	..	..	..			3 36	4 32	
GellyceidrimColl.Sdg.			..	..	..	..	..	..	..	..	..	..	..	..	..	..	..	..	..	..	..			—	—	—
GARNANT			..	..	..	..	..	..	..	..	..	..	..	..	..	..	..	..	..	..	..			**3 41**	4 37	
Gwaun-cae-GurwenC.	..	..	..	..	..	..	..	..	..	..	..	..	..	..	..	..	..	..	..	..	..			..	**4 52**	**5 40**
BRYNAMMAN WEST	..	..	..	..	..	..	..	..	..	..	..	..	..	..	..	..	..	..	..	..	..	..	..	**3 46**	..	..
Pantyffynnon North	—	—	—	—	—	..	..	..	—	—	**G**	..	..	..	..	See page 148.		—	—	See page 148.		..	..	..	..	..
Parcyrhun Halt	—	—	—	—	—	..	..	..	—	—		..	..	..	..			—	2 54			..	..	..	..	..
Tirydail	—	1 10	—	—	**1 16**	..	..	..	—	—	Light Engine.	..	..	..	..			2 56½	2 57			..	..	..	..	..
Llandebie	—	**N**—	1 X0		To Mountain Branch and return from Tirydail at 4.30 p.m.	..	..	..	2 55			..	..	..	..	..	..	3 2	3 2½	..	..	..	..	..	..	..
Cilyrychen Crossing	—	—	—	—		..	..	..	3 0X	3 10		..	..	..	..	..	..	—	—	3 0X	3 10	..	..	..	**H**	
Derwydd Road	1 19		1 6			..	..	..	See page 149.			..	..	..	..	1 6		3 6½	X3 7½	3 16X	3 28	..	..	..	1.15 p.m. Swansea (Vic.) to Llandovery **Freight. MX**	
Ffairfach	—	—				..	..	..			dep.	..	..	..	..	—	—	3 13½	3 14	—	—	..	..	..		
CARMARTHEN	..	..	See page 149.			..	..	..	..	..	p.m.	..	..	..	..	..	..	..	..	..	..	..	..	**C**		
Abergwili Junction	..	..				**H**		..	..	..	..	..	..	..	..	..	..	..	..	..	..	..	..	Empty C'ches. **SX**		
Abergwili			..	..		8.40 a.m. Swansea (Vic.) to Harlescott Sidings **Freight.**		..	..	..	..	..	..	..	..	..	..	..	..	..	..	..	..			
Nantgaredig	¶—Advertised depart 2.20 p.m.		..	..				..	..	..	..	..	..	..	..	..	..	..	..	..	..	..	..			
Llanarthney			..	..				..	..	..	..	..	..	..	..	..	..	..	..	..	..	..	..			
Dryslwyn			..	..				..	..	..	After banking 9.25 a.m. Stafford to Swansea (Vic.)	..	..	..	..	..	..	..	..	..	..	..	..			
Golden Grove			..	..				..	..	..		..	..	See page 147.		..	..	..	..	..	..	..	..		arr.	dep.
Llandilo Bridge	..	..	..	..				..	..	..		..	..			..	..	..	..	..	..	..	..	dep.	p.m.	p.m.
Carmarthen Valley Jct.	1 25		..	..	..	arr.	dep.	..	..	..		..	..	..	..	—	—	3 15		3 39		..	..	p.m.	See column four.	
LLANDILO	**1 27**	**1 29**	..	..	..	p.m.	p.m.	..	..	..		..	..	**1 4X**	**•2 6**	**1 18***	**X1 40**	**3 17X**	**3 18½**	**3 42X**	**3 55**	..	..	..		
Talley Road Halt	—	—	..	..	..	..	..	..	..	..		..	..	—	—	—	—	3 22½	3 23	—	—	..	..	..		
Glanrhyd Halt	—	—	..	..	..	..	..	..	..	..		..	..	—	—	—	—	3 27	3 27½	—	—	..	..	..		
Llangadock	—	1 39	..	..	..	..	..	..	..	..		..	..	2 19	X2 48	1 52		3 31	3 32	**4 8X**	**4 45**	..	..	4†30	4 8X	4 45
Llanwrda	—	1 43	..	..	..	..	..	..	..	..		..	..	2 56	X3 25	1 57		3 35½	X3 38	See column seven.		..	..	4 33	4 52X	4 54
LLANDOVERY	**1 49**	**1 54**	..	..	..	‡—Harlescott Sidings.		..	..	..		..	..	3 39	4 40	2 10E	T3 45	**3 45**	—			..	..	**4†39**	5 5	—
Cynghordy	—	X2 5	..	..	..			..	..	..	..	..	..	..	..	4 3		..	..			..	..	Sats. and School Holidays excepted.	..	..
Sugar Loaf Summit	2 15		..	..	..	..	..	..	..	..	..	..	..	..	..	4 23X	P4 30	..	..	..	..	..	..		..	..
Llanwrtyd Wells	2 19X	2¶25	..	..	..	See page 147.		..	..	..	..	..	..	..	..	4 38	P4 43	..	..	..	..	..	..		..	..
Llangammarch Wells	—	2 30	..	..	..			..	..	..	..	See page 146.		..	..	—	—	..	..	..	..	..	..		..	..
Garth	—	2 35	..	..	..	..	..	..	..	..	..			..	..	4 58	X5 10	..	..	..	..	..	..		..	..
Cilmery Halt	—	—	..	..	..	..	..	..	..	..	..			..	..	—	—	..	..	..	..	..	..		..	..
BUILTH ROAD (H.L.) ←«	**2 43**	**X2 45**	..	..	..	..	..	..	..	..	..	..	..	..	..	**5 25O**	**W5 35**	..	..	..	..	..	..		..	..
Howey	2 51		..	..	..	..	..	..	..	..	..	..	..	..	..	**5 49**	**X5 51**	..	..	..	..	..	..		..	..
LLANDRINDOD WELLS	**2 56**	**2 58**	..	..	..	..	..	..	..	..	..	**2 25X**	**3 35**	..	..	**6 1XC**	**D6 5**	..	..	..	..	..	..	..	..	..
Penybont	—	3 5	..	..	..	..	..	..	..	..	..	**3 45**	**4 20**	..	..	6 15		..	..	..	..	..	..	..	..	..
Penybont Junction	3 7		..	..	..	..	..	..	..	..	..	**4 22**		..	..	6 17		..	..	..	..	..	..	..	..	..
Dolau	—	3 12	..	..	..	..	..	..	..	..	..	**4 30**	**4 40**	..	..	—	—	..	..	..	..	..	..	..	..	..
Llanbister Road	—	3 20	..	..	..	**3 4X**	**3 28**	..	..	..	..	**4 50**	**X5 35**	..	..	6 31		..	..	..	..	..	..	..	..	..
Llangunllo	—	3 27	..	..	..	**3 38P**	**X3 43**	..	..	..	**5‖ 4**	**5 46**	**PX6*0**	..	..	**6 40X**	**P6 50**	..	..	..	..	..	..	..	..	..
Knucklas	—	3 34	..	..	..	—	—	..	..	..	—	**C**	**R**	..	..	—	—	..	..	..	..	..	..	..	..	..
KNIGHTON	**3 38**	**3 45**	..	..	..	**4 8CT**	**4P13**	..	..	..	**5‖16**	**6 25**	**6 40**	..	..	**7 15O**	**W7 27**	..	..	..	..	..	..	..	..	..
Bucknell	**3 51**	**3 53**	..	..	..	—	—	..	..	..	..	**6 50**	**7 10**	..	..	—	—	..	..	..	..	..	..	..	..	..
Hopton Heath	—	3 59	..	..	..	—	—	..	..	..	..	—	—	..	..	—	—	..	..	..	..	..	..	..	..	..
Broome	**4 4§**	**4 5**	..	..	..	—	—	..	..	..	..	—	—	..	..	—	—	..	..	..	..	..	..	..	..	..
CRAVEN ARMS	**4 17§**	**4 20**	..	..	..	**4 43C**	**R4*55**	..	..	..	..	**7 30**	—	..	..	**C7 56R**		..	..	..	..	..	..	..	..	..
Shrewsbury	**5 2**	—	..	..	..	**6‡10**	—	..	..	..	..	..	..	..	..	**9¶ 1**	—	..	..	..	..	..	..	..	..	..

EXPLANATION OF GENERAL NOTES.

- ● Shunt for, or follow another train, and also to perform work.
- • Shunt for, or follow another train, but not to perform work.
- × Train crosses another on single line.
- ‖ Light Engine.
- † Empty Train, or Auto Car, or Engine and Van.
- **BE** Attach or detach Bank Engine. ‡
- **CD** Change Enginemen. ‡
- **CE** Change Engines. ‡
- **CG** Change Guards. ‡
- **CR** Call when required.
- **CS** Call at Single Line Stations for Train Staff, Tablet, Token or Ticket. ‡
- **CT** Change Enginemen and Guards. ‡
- **EG** Change Engines and Guards. ‡
- **EO** Stop for Examination. ‡
- **ET** Stop for Examination and Traffic purposes.
- **EW** Stop for Examination and Water. ‡
- **F** Fridays. ¶
- **L** Stop if required to detach traffic. ‡
- **LO** Change Head Codes ‡
- **M** Mondays. ¶
- **OW** Stop for Water. ‡
- **P** Stop dead here.
- **Q** Stop if required to attach Traffic.
- **RR** Run when required only.
- **S** Saturdays. ¶
- **ST** Calls when required for Station Truck Work. ‡
- **T** Tuesdays. ¶
- **T** *Without* **O** or **X** added, indicates **" Collect Tickets."**
- **Th** Thursdays. ¶
- **W** Wednesdays. ¶

¶ These letters, singly or in combination, with the addition of O or X, indicate " .... days only (or excepted)," e.g., **TO** Tuesdays only, **FX** Fridays excepted, **MWFO** Mondays, Wednesdays and Fridays only, **ThSX** Thursdays and Saturdays excepted.

‡ These notes are used only when trains are required to stop for the specific purpose indicated.

↞ Stations or Signal Boxes marked thus denote the Boundary between one District and another. Shewick Junction, Red Hill Junction and Builth Road are in the Chester District.

The small figures thus (7.30) show the times of passing the Stations.

Figures in italics thus (*7.30*) refer to trains which only run occasionally.

LIST OF REFUGE SIDINGS AND RUNNING LOOPS—continued.

	From	To	Refuge Sidings.	Running Loops.	Number of Wagons Siding or Loop holds.‡
	SWANSEA (Victoria), LLANELLY DOCK, LLANDOVERY AND CRAVEN ARMS (exclusive).				
Up and Down.	Knighton	—	1	—	45
Up.	Llangunllo	—	1	—	49
	Penybont	—	1	—	33
Up and Down.	Llandrindod Wells	—	1	—	60
Up.	Pantyffynnon South	Pantyffynnon North	1	—	37
	Pontardulais Junction Station ..	Pontardulais Junction North ..	—	1	68
	Morlais Junction	—	—	1	62
	Llangennech Siding	—	—	1	56
Down.	Swansea Bay	—	1	—	33
	Dunvant	—	1	—	50
	Morfa Junction	—	—	1	35
	Llangennech Station ..	—	—	1	72
	Pontardulais Junction North ..	Pontardulais Junction Station ..	—	1	44
	Pantyffynnon North	Pantyffynnon South	—	1	50
†	Tirydail	—	—	1	40
†	Llandebie	—	—	1	45
†	Cilyrychen Crossing	—	—	1	32
†	Llangadock	—	1	—	40
	Llandovery	—	1	—	24
	PANTYFFYNNON AND BRYNAMMAN WEST.				
Up	Pantyffynnon	—	—	1	71
Down.	Pantyffynnon	—	—	1	57
„	Pantyffynnon	—	—	1	57
„	Ammanford Colliery	—	—	1	63
„ †	Glanamman	—	—	1	67

‡—Capacity based on length of wagons as 21 feet, in addititiion to engine and van.

†—Available for Down and Up Trains.